P9-BVM-498

PORTRAITS OF PRODUCTIVE SCHOOLS

SUNY Series in Science Education
Robert E. Yager, editor

PORTRAITS OF PRODUCTIVE SCHOOLS

An International Study of Institutionalizing Activity-Based Practices in Elementary Science

Uwe Hameyer
Jan van den Akker
Ronald D. Anderson
Mats Ekholm

State University of New York Press

Published by
State University of New York Press, Albany

Printed in the United States of America

For information, address the State University of New York Press, State University Plaza, Albany, NY 12246

Production by Christine Lynch
Marketing by Nancy Farrell

Library of Congress Cataloging-in-Publication Data

Portraits of productive schools : an international study of institutionalizing activity-based practices in elementary science / by Uwe Hameyer . . . [et al.].
p. cm. — (SUNY series in science education)
Includes bibliographical references and index.
ISBN 0-7914-2499-5 (alk. paper). — ISBN 0-7914-2500-2 (pbk. : alk. paper)
1. Science—Study and teaching (Elementary)—Cross-cultural studies. 2. Science—Study and teaching—Activity programs—Cross-cultural studies. I. Hameyer, Uwe. II. Series.
LB1585.P67 1995
372.3′5—dc20 94-31526
CIP

10 9 8 7 6 5 4 3 2 1

Contents

Preface

The big issues in education tend to be universal, that is, they cut across national, social and cultural boundaries. What knowledge is of most worth? How should it be taught? How does one go about changing educational institutions to make them more consistent with the answers to such questions? Given the pervasiveness of these issues, it has been fascinating for us as researchers from four different countries to collaborate on an international study of forward-looking science instruction in elementary schools.

Questions about the desired character of education and how to change schooling to bring it more in line with this desired state are at the heart of the research addressed in this book. In particular, we have conducted case studies in four different countries—Germany, the Netherlands, Sweden, and the United States—of schools which have made activity-based science instruction an integral part of their ongoing programs for 9- and 10-year-old children.

We have come to this endeavor with varied perspectives—not just the perspectives of different countries, but of different professional backgrounds as well. In some cases, a predominant influence has been past work in a particular science subject; in others, it has been experience in a general curriculum and instructional context; and in other instances, it has been the study of schools as changing social institutions. The sharing of these perspectives has enriched our collaboration as we have studied schools and fashioned portraits of their productive efforts in science.

The first major question of interest to us here—that pertaining to the desired character of science education for elementary-aged children—is one on which we have taken a position. We have chosen to identify as exemplary practice, and to portray here in case studies, what we are calling "activity-based science." Although this label will be defined in greater detail later, it may be well to note here that we are not referring to activity simply for the sake of activity, but to an intellectual endeavor that addresses essential concepts and modes of investigation in science. A label many others have used—"hands-on, minds-on" science education—would be consistent with our answer to this fundamental question of the desired character of education. It is also consistent with such approaches as open education and child-centered teaching.

Even though we have taken a position on this question by virtue of how we have designed our case study investigations, it is well to note that the question of the desired character of education is not closed. It is a matter of intense ongoing discussion in many circles, as it has been for generations. All of us have been participants in these discussions, and each of us has previously been deeply involved in curriculum studies that have encompassed very specific responses to this issue. It is not our purpose to resolve this debate in this book, but we will note some of the current dialogue as a backdrop for our work.

The second major question—that of how schools can change to more fully exhibit the desired form of education—is also of universal concern, although it has only recently become a topic of intensive scholarly investigation. As in the case of the first question, all of us have been involved in prior research on this topic in a variety of contexts.

The research reported in this book was initiated at the behest of the German member of our group—Uwe Hameyer—who managed the overall endeavor. He began the project with a meeting he hosted for us at the Institute for Science Education (IPN) in Kiel (Germany). The meeting took place shortly after completion at IPN of AKTIF (Hameyer, Dudek, Friis & Hameyer, 1992), a new science curriculum for 7- to 13-year-old pupils. AKTIF uses an integrated approach to exploring nature, combined with the development of basic mathematical skills and students' use of language and writing, with the primary aim of developing improved instruction and activity-based learning through discovery. During the implementation of AKTIF, it became apparent that more systematic knowledge for curriculum renewal was needed in order to insure maintenance of activity-based elementary science practices. Having faced the challenges in other countries of implementing innovative educational practice in various science-education settings—as well as other educational settings—the others of us in this team were most willing to enter into a collaborative project.

Together we developed the conceptual framework and research design for a set of case studies to be conducted by ourselves and colleagues in our four countries. The ensuing research was conducted under the project name of IMPACT, derived from the longer designation, *Implementing Activity-Based Learning in Elementary Science Teaching*. Fifteen case studies were conducted. All are contained in a technical report available from the IPN in Kiel (Ekholm, et al., 1995). The studies concern productive processes of enduring curriculum renewal as carried out on the elementary school level.

In this book we present the design of this research, the educational context of the four countries, and sample cases, as well as generalizations from cross-case analysis and recommendations for practice. At the core of this book is a description of exemplary practices. The cases are analyzed with particular attention to change processes. We have concentrated on mapping out what productive schools have in common.

Although the major findings refer to the domain of elementary science teaching, the potential impact goes well beyond this arena. Our intent is to illustrate how to create schools where students learn to explore unknown phenomena, to gain knowledge from active participation in the instructional process, and to organize their own learning activities so that intrinsic motivation is more likely to occur.

Our intended audience for this book includes teachers, principals, support personnel, policy-makers, and school authorities, as well as researchers who want to gain insight into the workings of a self-renewing school where innovative instructional practices, such as activity-based learning in science, survive and gradually become routinized educational work. More specifically, the book is for all who are curious about *activity-based learning in elementary science teaching* and how to put it into practice; our cases stem from this field of educational practice. In our final chapter we evaluate the findings and propose practical recommendations for instructional development and school renewal. Some recommendations pertain to activity-based learning in elementary science teaching; others transcend this domain. We are attempting to show in an authentic and illustrative way how innovative activity profiles emerge and secure a continuing position in the school curriculum, instructional practice, staff development, principals' expectations and support, district policy, and other areas.

We have conducted this research work along with our ongoing professional responsibilities; we have not had external funding to relieve us of other responsibilities in order to devote ourselves exclusively to this work. As a result, we owe a debt of thanks to a large number of individuals and institutions. An early consultant to the project was Karl Frey, then Director of IPN and now Professor of Education at the Swiss University Institute of Technology in Zurich. Matthew B. Miles, Senior Researcher at the Institute for Policy Research, Tappan, New York, has given helpful feedback on our work. The institutions with which we are affiliated have been very supportive. The IPN has been a mainstay of the project, and has provided support of several kinds as have the University of Twente (the Netherlands), Karlstad University (Sweden), and the University of Colorado (U.S.A.). The National Science Foundation supported the travel expenses of several researchers from the United States under its Cooperative Research Program.

The largest debt of thanks, however, is owed to researchers from two countries who, in addition to ourselves, conducted or assisted in conducting the several case studies on which this work is based: Kirsten Lindvall in Sweden and James Gallagher, Beth Hower, Carol Mitchener, Deborah Muscella, and Kenneth Tobin in the United States. Many thanks are also due to the people in the many schools which were the subjects of our case studies. These many people must remain anonymous, however; all of our cases use pseudonyms for the schools and their personnel.

While the contributions of these people were numerous and extensive, the responsibility for inadequacies in what is reported in this book will obviously have to rest with us. We hope that this research provides for the readers many of the insights we have gained in our work together.

Uwe Hameyer
Jan van den Akker
Ronald Anderson
Mats Ekholm
Bjørstorp, Sweden
August 29, 1993

Chapter 1

Learning from Productive Schools

In its broadest sense, this book is about the "biographies" of 15 productive elementary schools in Germany, the Netherlands, Sweden, and the United States. The selected schools are called "productive" because they show—each in its own unique way—that learning can be enriched by a culture of effective educational creativity in schools partly designed as open learning communities. The development of new ideas to raise instructional quality is informally expected to be a major task of any reflective practitioner (cf. Schon, 1991).

It goes without saying that internal productivity and creativity require external support—a matter that will be addressed in what follows. Yet the core of this book is about what happens *inside* a productive school and what makes its patterns of practice particularly attractive. This includes school-based initiatives to acquire external support or advice.

Defining a Productive School

The term "productive" encompasses more than intellectual curiosity, creative thought, or arguing for an exciting initiative in one's own school. We conceive of a school as a productive organization if it succeeds in putting a shared innovative idea into lasting practice. "Productive" means working effectively to implement *and* institutionalize the idea or vision. It means to reinvent *and* to protect something new against traditional routine; to develop implementation procedures *and* to try them out repeatedly; to give "fuzzy" ideas a chance to emerge *and* to support their elaboration; to learn how to master the new *and* to cooperate with others so that experiences can be exchanged and efforts mutually supported.

We felt it necessary to study the processes inside a school that encourage the teaching staff to provide and extend opportunities for activity-based learning. A cross-case comparison of successful practices in several countries was also considered necessary. We initiated an internationally-oriented design to reconstruct and compare the biographies of elementary schools where activity-based practices endured. We were interested in both the character of the science instruction and the means by which it was sustained over time.

This project allowed researchers from four countries to examine the lasting implementation of hands-on science activities in elementary schools: What was the nature of the science education which took place? What were the outcomes for students? How were activity-based approaches effectively continued? What was done to encourage and support self-renewal inside the schools? As the research developed, the emphasis shifted more and more to the *process of sustained productive renewal*.

By looking at productive schools, we have had the opportunity to see what *really works in practice*. The insights gained have the potential of helping others see how to go from a vision of what is desired to creating programs in which the vision becomes reality.

TWO FACES OF THE STUDY

We are playing, so to speak, with two balls at the same time: one is the *science activity domain* and the other is the *school improvement domain*. Both are strongly intertwined; our book is about the nature of this interplay. Before attending specifically to how these two domains are addressed in our case studies, however, some background information is relevant.

The nature of elementary science education

Although the nature of teaching and learning in science for children is of long standing interest, during the last third-of-a-century it has received intense and sustained attention, both in a theoretical sense and in the development of classroom materials. Examples of significant innovative published materials can be seen in three of the four countries which are part of this research. AKTIF, the program recently developed at IPN in Germany is an example. It uses an integrated approach to exploring nature, combined with the development of basic mathematical skills and students' use of language and writing; its primary aim is to develop improved instruction and activity-based learning through discovery.

The major example of an elementary science education curriculum from the Netherlands is the NOB project of the National Institute for

Curriculum Development (SLO). It is centered on integrating major elements of the science subject-matter domain, including biology, chemistry and physics, and is intended to foster an activity-based approach to learning science. The United States has seen substantial activity in this area as well, beginning in the 1960s with projects such as the Elementary Science Study (ESS), Science—A Process Approach (SAPA), and Science Curriculum Improvement Study (SCIS), which were developed with funding from the government's National Science Foundation. Similar funding has created a new generation of such projects in the current decade.

Both practical curriculum development work and theoretical analysis raise many questions, most of which are not new but are of continuing interest. Examples include the following:

- Which science concepts and core educational ideas are of greatest value to children?
- To what extent should an understanding of the nature of scientific investigation be a curricular goal?
- To what extent should this understanding be pursued in the context of technology- and science-related societal issues?
- To what extent is science learning best pursued in an activity-based manner?

School improvement: another focus of concern

In addition to our focus on the nature of elementary school science education, the means by which school change and improvement come about is of major interest. Again, this topic is not new. Experience has shown that the science-curriculum work described above has not had the full impact on school practice that was originally intended. Many questions arise as to why this is so. Research on this topic has been noteworthy, but questions such as the following remain:

- To what extent is it possible for science curricula to be developed external to a school and then imported into the school setting?
- What assistance do teachers generally need to initiate curricular change?
- How significant to the adoption of activity-based science education are the problems of providing student materials?
- To what extent can curricular change be initiated in a centralized manner and to what extent must it be decentralized to the individual school level?
- To what extent is change restricted by teacher beliefs and values or by cultural or institutional barriers?

PROJECT IMPACT

Our case studies provide insights into questions such as those raised above. By looking at schools where activity-based learning in science exists, and by understanding some of the history of how these schools reached this point, it is possible to gain some understanding of how other schools could move to a similar position.

At the same time that this potential is being noted, it is well to acknowledge that this research does *not* provide definitive answers to the full set of such questions, or even to those given as examples above. The project was not designed with such a purpose as its goal. It is interpretive research; the intent was to look at productive schools in considerable detail for the insights that could be gained about elementary school science education. It is also comparative research; it compares cultures and learning processes on the elementary school level.

Along with this disclaimer, however, we want to promise to return to these questions, since it is largely such questions that make the research of interest. In the analysis provided later, such matters will reappear. It will then be time to address the *relevance* of such questions, which may be of greater or lesser interest within different national contexts.

SCHOOL BIOGRAPHIES

With the school as the unit of analysis, the knowledge provided and experiences related in this book to some extent—as noted at the beginning of this chapter—have the character of biographies of the 15 schools. They reveal how fragile innovative efforts can be and what is needed to anchor them in the culture of a school.

Researchers are recognizing that—particularly in science studies—educational research should more vigorously pursue research questions such as the following:

> How are reform initiatives enculturated into to the process of schooling? What are the impediments to reform, as well as the constraints upon the implementation of a reformed curriculum? What constitutes reasonable measures of successful curriculum reform? (Shymansky & Kyle, 1991, p. 17)

Questions of this nature are the focus of concern for our research. The process of *enculturation*—of building the new into the setting called "school"—occurred step by step in all the IMPACT cases. Our study is about the process of enculturation and its dependence upon mutual learning and competency development. In view of this specification, our key question can be stated as follows: *What makes sustained improvement in elementary school science happen over the long run*?

Our major concern was to study in depth what these schools actually did to create an effective and motivating learning environment and an active culture of cooperation and school-based development. We were less interested in looking at doubtful short-term success, and particularly interested in portraying innovative practice profiles which lasted for more than a year or two.

In developing such portraits, and in gaining insights into the cultures of individual schools (Sarason, 1971), we focused our analysis on the specific subject of science—including technology—and sought to better understand the life of an innovative effort until it was finally institutionalized. As activity-based learning methods are internationally accepted as a key to increased quality in science education, we chose to study these methods as displayed within the real curricular and instructional practices of schools. This international acceptance is backed by empirical research. In the United States, for example, meta-analyses conducted by Shymanksy, Kyle and Alport (1983) and by Bredderman (1983) both point clearly to increased learning for elementary school science instruction based on activities using manipulative materials. (Walberg, 1991, p. 46) concluded that the "new" science courses "produced superior learning on tests of their intended outcomes, and they often produced no worse learning on traditional achievement tests of science content." We observed classroom work, as well as instructional activities conducted outside the classroom, with particular attention to activity-based learning in the sciences for 9- to 10-year-old children.

Although the findings were analyzed with the school as the unit of analysis, a district organizational level was involved in some cases as well. The focus was on the schools, not on national systems; we summarized the activity patterns the schools have in common—and the practical knowledge they provide—for others who seek to improve schools and to create productive learning environments.

A Reconstructive View

We follow a *reconstructive* model of analysis. Particularly in the domain of instructional research and school improvement, investigators still often prefer to pursue the what-is-missing issue instead of asking why specific new ways of mastering educational demands grow and gain power. We consider learning from such new ways to be as helpful as the analysis of problems at hand. Reconstructing the conditions under which sustained improvement occurs is the specific strategy which we apply. We analyze why it is that carefully selected productive schools were able to institutionalize activity-based learning in elementary science teaching: What did they do on the school and classroom level? And what can we conclude from the interplay of these levels of practice?

Much past research attends to these issues. Walberg (1984) claims evidence that high quality instruction has a paramount impact on learning results. On the instructional level, he investigates the influence of open education on student learning. Drawing upon the meta-analysis studies of Hedges, Giaconia & Gage (1981), and Raven (1981), he concludes that "students in open classes do not do worse in standardized achievement and do slightly better on several outcomes that educators, parents, and students hold to be of great value" (Walberg, 1984, p. 25). In this context, Walberg refers to cooperativeness, creativity, independence, lifelong learning abilities, self-reliance, and critical thinking.

So we considered it necessary to study the instructional practice profiles of our schools in depth. We went to the schools and observed many lessons. We interviewed teachers, principals and students, and analyzed documents and school curricula. In order to gain the needed objectivity and to have a basis for making comparisons across many school sites, a conceptual framework and a variety of research protocols were developed. The methodological foundations of this multi-method, multi-site approach are described in the following chapter. This strong analytical base provides a foundation for an expectation of valid understandings of the conditions under which innovative efforts are more likely to occur *and* to survive.

We gained new insights into long-term institutionalization of school-based innovations. The majority of evaluation studies of school improvement have been limited to the analysis of short-term effects. We thought it much more realistic to study long-lasting efforts which finally become part of daily school life. Our camera focuses on the various faces of innovative practices, particularly on the processes of *initiation, implementation, and institutionalization* within a school.

Chapter 2

IMPACT: A Cross-National Study

Everybody who reflects on schools and how they work certainly has an image of what is good and what could be better. And in hundreds of empirical studies, researchers have studied means by which improvements could occur. Among others: the DESSI study (Crandall & Loucks, 1983); the evaluation of innovation projects by Louis (1983); the dissemination analysis of Emrick & Peterson (1978); and the International School Improvement Project (ISIP) by (van Velzen, Miles, Ekholm, Hameyer & Robin, 1985) have addressed these means.

HORIZON: LONG-TERM IMPROVEMENT OF SCHOOLS

If we decide to seek long-term improvement in elementary science in a school or schools, which of many paths or combinations of paths do we take? What do we already know about the nature of interactions that enable schools to sustain renewal? How do these interactions induce or impede each other? Such concerns have often been raised by parents, policy-makers, teachers and authorities alike. Research on sustained school improvement has thus received growing attention from policymakers, researchers, and practitioners.

When the specific curricular focus of the change endeavor is science, the more detailed questions reflect the character of this subject matter and its interaction with the school context: To what extent is the change process different from what it would be with other subject areas? (For example, does the need for fairly numerous learning materials pose formidable challenges?) Is the challenge of maintaining substantial curricular attention to science significantly more difficult when integrating science with other instruction, as studies in Canada suggest (Schoeneberger & Russell, 1986)? To what extent is teachers' ability to make the desired changes influenced by their level of science background? What are the merits of externally developed curriculum materials and their related student manipulative materials as compared to curricula developed by teachers within a local school? To what extent can or should change strategies for elementary science be "top-down" or "bottom-up?"

Much of the research on change has addressed innovations which lasted for less than a year, or even for only a few months (cf. Gross, Giacquinta & Bernstein, 1971; Keith & Smith, 1971; Berman, et al., 1975; and Galton, Simon & Croll, 1980). Substantial research is needed on long-term change and the conditions under which these changes are likely to be sustained over periods of years (see Miles, Ekholm & Vandenberghe 1987).

In the IMPACT research project, we wanted to investigate how lasting efforts are effectively sustained. In contrast to earlier studies or reviews, we wanted to focus on multiple-year changes and the concept of institutionalization elaborated by Miles (1983) and Miles, Ekholm & Vandenberghe (1987) in studying long-term change processes (cf. Gaynor & Clauset, 1985).

A school is much too complex and culturally framed to give room for instantaneous renewal. Meaningful conceptual frameworks, multiple tryouts, reflective feedback and steady support are needed over long periods of time to attain success. Practitioners in the schools seek clear control over the right to ascertain whether the innovation is sufficiently practical, meaningful and appropriate for the classroom. Only on such premises are teachers ready to adjust familiar patterns and routines to new demands in a lasting way. Achieving this result requires local creativity and school-based involvement. The talents and energies of teachers and others are primary resources. Yet, how are such essentials attained inside individual schools? And what lessons can we draw from successful cases?

These open questions stimulated us to investigate schools where significant improvement efforts had lasted over a period of years. Learning from such productive schools about the forces that foster improvement became our major research focus.

Choice: Case-Study Technique

The schools chosen for study were highly productive but had achieved this status without special resources from outside the schools or from the local districts of which they were a part. We wanted to study how a school working under the usual burden of daily tasks implements its own initiatives.

Sites were chosen which were said to be highly productive according to the assessment of informants who were knowledgeable about the schools. After a careful series of telephone and letter inquiries, we talked with the principal of each proposed school to find out whether activity-based learning in science had lasted more than 2 years and if it was well anchored in the daily life of the school. With this information, we then selected a limited number of schools on which in-depth case studies were to be conducted using a common research format. It should be noted that it was not very easy to find schools that met these criteria.

Focus: Activity-Based Learning

Our investigation focused on activity-based learning in general science studies. We looked for efforts wherein a substantial percentage of the teaching staff had reduced teacher-directed patterns of class teaching in favor of hands-on activities, self-guided discovery, and doing one's own experiments—either individually or in cooperation with other students in the class.

A major reason to study activity-based learning practices in science comes from the results of classroom research. Top-down patterns of teacher-focused instruction seem to prevent students from active learning and, even more, from learning *how* to learn (Dreeben 1973). In such instruction, teachers usually put from one to four questions per minute to the students (Hoetker & Ahlbrand, 1969). Adam and Biddle (1970) report that at least 75% of instructional time is traditionally spent on teacher-centered instruction in which the focus is on academic knowledge. Bellack et al. (1966) found that teachers talk three times as much as pupils during lessons and use "rapid-fire questioning." Only 7% of the teachers' talking time is devoted to the students' questions. "The rest consists of asking questions, focusing pupils' attention on topics, and commenting on and judging what they say" (Dreeben, 1973, p. 465, referring to Bellack, et al., 1966, pp. 43 & 47). Student initiative is not encouraged by such practices, which generally create passive orientation patterns toward learning (Koumin, 1970). It is noteworthy that these typical patterns were reconfirmed in the large scale study of Goodlad (1984).

More recently, many of these issues have been addressed under the banner of *constructivism*. Although this widely-used label has varied meanings, it is generally understood to include the following ideas: First, learning depends upon the prior conceptions that the learner brings to the classroom. Each individual has his or her own unique network of prior beliefs and knowledge structures. Second, the learner must construct her or his own meaning, as suggested by some philosophers for a long time and more recently elaborated by the results of cognitive research. Third, learning is contextual; our understandings are dependent upon the particular contexts in which they develop. Finally, learning is dependent upon shared understandings negotiated with others. The importance of this shared meaning has major implications for the choice of classroom activities, modes of discussion, forms of cooperative learning, and other classroom practices (Anderson, et al., 1992).

Our experiences with elementary school science curriculum change endeavors in all of our countries (e.g., AKTIF in Germany, NOB in the Netherlands, and ESS, SAPA, and SCIS in the United States) have raised many implementation issues. While exploring these issues, it has become apparent that more systematic knowledge is needed to better prepare for maintaining activity-based elementary science practices over time.

In conducting the research, we first had to define activity-based learning. As defined here, *activity-based learning* is a pattern of science learning having the following components:

1. The pupils develop their own ideas for inquiries, experiments or constructive work. They search for explorative methods to clarify and illuminate the questions which they consider meaningful.
2. Students investigate meaningful questions or problems on the basis of their own ideas. They explore their ideas and apply different methods.
3. Students analyze, discuss and evaluate what they have found or constructed; they display their results in the classroom or other places.
4. Students express their understanding of what they have learned. They exchange findings or constructive results, and they draw conclusions where possible and appropriate.

This conceptual framework encompasses various hands-on activities and learning materials such as books, direct exploration of nature, personal interaction, and information resources both within and outside the school. The patterns of activity-based learning in science embedded in these methods and materials are expected to:

- provide semi-structured opportunities for students to interact with materials in a multi-sensory way (i.e., observing, constructing, experimenting with equipment, reading, listening carefully, interacting with other students, and equivalent activities);

- relate to basic issues of science and technology that are educationally meaningful and allow substantial room for students to build on prior ideas and perceptions of phenomena;
- facilitate the student's capacity to discover and learn by doing an experiments or other activities;
- allow students to plan and conduct experiments and activities, and grow in the self-direction of their learning;
- allow room for various hands-on activities, such as experimenting with simple equipment, doing investigations, learning games, and going on field visits.

The extent and quality of the above elements may vary, but the programs and practices selected for this study should meet these points to a substantial degree.

The ultimate goal of such educational efforts is to ensure that students develop the scientific literacy for self-empowerment, social empowerment, citizenship, and social responsibility (cf. Shymansky & Kyle, 1991; Hameyer, in press; Wallrabenstein, 1991). Content-oriented science activities are closely interrelated with fundamental educational goals. Therefore we see the domain of science teaching as an integral part of instruction and of the school where learning takes place.

ELABORATION: DIMENSIONS OF ACTIVITY-BASED LEARNING IN SCIENCE

Given the above understanding of activity-based learning in science, one can address more directly the ways in which it is reflected in the schools which are a part of this research study. This approach to learning is reflected in these schools through their programs, the teachers involved, the processes employed, and the broader context, as elaborated below.

Program

The pedagogical program must be considered from at least two perspectives. The first is a *description* of the program or curriculum being used in a school, including the sequence of units, pedagogical principles of the curriculum, content characteristics, and the time devoted to various aspects. The second is the *perception* of the program or curriculum from the perspective of the teachers and others involved in conducting the program. These perceptions include not only sequence, pedagogical principles, content, and time, but also such matters as the program's relevance, credibility, utility and availability, as well as the problems associated with fostering learning among the unique group of students found in a particular school. Other considerations include ease of use (or lack thereof) and the program's connection to other aspects of the total curriculum and general school life. While the descriptive aspect can be determined by objective review of documents and observation of activities, the perceptual aspect is determined largely by interviews with teachers and school leaders.

Persons

The teachers themselves obviously portray the program and their own ideas through their actions and attitudes in the classroom. In the course of our study, both observations and interviews came into play as the researchers sought to understand teachers' knowledge and beliefs concerning activity-based learning, their preparation for engaging students in such work, and their skill in putting it all into practice.

Context

The program is also a reflection of the context in which it is conducted—in particular, the culture and social climate of the school (Morgan, 1993 and Fullan, 1993). A mismatch between contextual demands and activity-based learning can potentially be high, with a resulting low use of the activity-based program if such factors are disregarded or their degree of impact underestimated. Organizational theory and school improvement research indicate the importance of researchers attending to such matters as: the climate for innovation in the school; the degree of collaboration within the school as well as between the school and the community; the stability or turnover of the staff; community "ownership" of the school; and school commitment to activity-based learning in science.

Process

The process by which activity-based learning comes into the school and becomes an integral part of school life is also key. Mastery by teachers and institutionalization (becoming an integral part of the culture of the school) are also part of determining whether or not the desired approach to science learning is seen in the lives of students.

RATIONALE: LEARNING FROM SUCCESS

Although there is considerable research evidence that activity-based elementary science is more effective than traditional science teaching, it has been shown that the use of activity-based learning is not common school practice (Stake & Easley, 1978; Yager & Penick, 1983; Harlen, 1985) and that teachers are strongly inclined not to use this form of instruction frequently (Schoeneberger & Russell, 1986). Since the focus of our research was to be on putting such instruction into practice, we chose to study "good" examples (i.e., schools where such practices had found their way into sustained practice). We elaborated a design to clarify why, in certain cases, teachers and students *succeeded* in putting such innovative approaches into sustained practice. Learning from practical improvement became a core focus. While there is also a recent, interesting line of research on learning from "exemplary" teachers (Berliner, 1986; Fraser, Tobin & Lacy, 1988; Shulman, 1986), our IMPACT study has a somewhat broader scope, describing the teacher and learner activities within the context of the school as an organization.

Investigating this issue in a comparative way was partially inspired by the OECD's International School Improvement Project (ISIP) in which plans were developed for cooperative efforts regarding institutionalizing school renewal (cf. Van Velzen, Miles, Ekholm, Hameyer & Vandenberghe, 1985; and Miles, Ekholm & Vandenberghe, 1987). Preliminary outlines for a common research project were drafted with the expectation that cross-country knowledge could contribute substantially to identifying basic conditions under which activity-based practices are more likely to occur and to be maintained. The plans finally developed included the study of activity-based science learning in three to six schools in each country.

SCOPE: RESEARCH QUESTIONS FOR INVESTIGATION

The main research questions formulated for investigation included the following:

1. What is the activity-based pattern of learning and instruction in these particular successful schools?
2. How did the pedagogical pattern enter the school?
3. How did staff and students in the school get acquainted with the new pattern?
4. How did the internal users and supporters adopt and implement the new approaches?

5. What indicates the beginning of institutionalized use?

6. What was the flow of events after the beginning of institutionalization?

METHODOLOGY: CROSS-SITE COMPARISON

The IMPACT study represents a complex empirical approach with an emphasis on qualitative data analysis. It includes attention to the context under study as perceived by the participants in it (see Yin, 1984). The methodology utilizes systematic, cross-case analysis of data acquired using a common case-study format, and data-analysis procedures developed by Miles and Huberman (1984):

> In a multiple-site study be certain that all field workers understand each question and see its importance. Multiple-site studies have to be more explicit so that site researchers can be aligned as they collect information in the field. Poor alignment—unclear questions, different understandings—makes for noncomparable data across cases (Miles & Huberman, 1984, p. 36).

Exploratory reasoning in a cross-site study is not limited to the identification of important factors or indicators of lasting school renewal. In this approach we make cross-case comparisons of coincident requirements for institutionalizing activity-based learning in science. In this way we identify the simultaneous occurrence of indicators which are crucial during the particular stages of school improvement.

The explorative logic of the reasoning in our study draws upon grounded theory. In view of the strong variations across the different countries and educational systems, we are not so much concerned with universal generalizations as we are with finding formulations of concrete knowledge that apply in identifiable situations. Studying 15 cases on an in-depth level over an extended period provides sufficient grounds for the stability of such findings. This method offers more than what Eisner (1979) calls "educational connoisseurship" since we have built into the study the following opportunities for control and feedback:

- a relatively large number of cases;
- cross-evaluation by four researchers;
- checking of cases by all interviewees;
- feedback from independent experts;
- wide variation across a number of countries, which gives strong validity to common features across the cases;
- five sessions of repeated cross-case comparison involving the four researchers at different points in times during the research process.

The qualitative method applied in the IMPACT study traces back to the hermeneutic technique of discerning categories—which allows for explanatory understanding of complex reality—while at the same time empirical field-work methods such as interviewing, observation and other procedures are used to specify comparable knowledge across the cases. For the empirical part of our study we have developed a conceptual framework to apply to all the cases and case-study writing so that comparison is supported.

Instruments

Standard qualitative instruments were used (i.e., protocols for interviews and classroom observations to acquire information related to the research questions identified above). The researchers developed these protocols jointly for various dimensions of each research question to be used in interview and observation contexts. Interviews were conducted with the help of a common interview guide.

Data collection and analysis

The researchers compiled data in three forms during site visits, as follows.

Field notes. During visits to classes, and throughout observation in the schools, the researchers made notations of observations. Standard procedures for making notes available as feedback to teachers were followed.

Interim generalizations. The researchers prepared written notes of inferences, exploratory findings, impressions gained, and embryonic generalizations which deserved testing during subsequent interviews with teachers and other personnel.

Interviews. The researchers conducted interviews with teachers, principals and other key personnel who are part of the process of practicing or supporting activity-based science learning. With permission, interviews were sometimes recorded and transcribed later to facilitate data collection. An iterative process of interviewing makes it possible to explore new questions and test emerging generalizations through repeated interviews.

Data analysis occurred both during and following data collection. As is reflected in the description of data collection above, some analysis occurred on an ongoing basis, with the results influencing subsequent data collection. Upon conclusion of the data collection, data analysis continued in preparation for writing a case-study report for each case.

To assist data analysis for each case—and to aid subsequent cross-case analysis—a number of tentative data display formats were prepared ahead of time by the group of researchers as suggested by Miles and Huberman (1984). An example of such a display, to profile perceived characteristics of the curriculum in a school, is presented below.

DIMENSION	DESCRIPTION	RATING (H,M,L)	REMARKS
Accessibility			
Attractiveness			
Demandingness			
Practicality			
Centrality			
Curriculum fit			

Although valuable for the data analysis done for each case, the most important reason for such displays—and the data collection protocols used to get the needed data—was to insure that comparable information was available for the subsequent cross-site analyses.

Cross-site analysis

Upon completion of the individual case studies conducted in the four countries, the researchers were in a position to do a cross-site analysis in accordance with the conceptual framework developed at the beginning of the research. The data collection and analysis procedures for the individual cases described above were developed with subsequent cross-site analyses in mind. Initial analysis was done across sites within countries, followed by analyses that cut across all cases and countries.

Reporting the results of the cross-site analysis

The results of the cross-site analysis are reported in chapter 9 in accordance with a process model of the incorporation of an innovation into a school, as suggested by past school improvement research and validated in this study. The report follows a process model which is divided into overlapping stages of movement toward institutionalization.

These stages are analytically constructed. They are not expected to occur in distinct isolation; the stages are interactive and to some extent each one overlaps the subsequent stage. The types of questions addressed in this analysis pertaining to each stage are illustrated by the listings below.

Initiation. Why is it that activity-based learning in science has gained growing interest and initial commitment in the school? How did it happen? How did the teachers and the principal, the students and the parents, the authorities and the support professionals get acquainted with the new outlook after the initiative was in place? What did they decide to do to promote further steps and tryouts? Which elements of activity-based learning were selected? Which requirements had to be developed and which patterns of established practice had to be attuned? What was achieved by exploratory tryouts?

Implementation. Who was involved after the exploratory phase, and in what way? How was the implementation process designed in terms of time, personnel, resources and support? To what extent did the staff start to reconstruct previous practices and regulations? Which models for practice could be further elaborated and implemented? Which characteristics indicate that the teachers and students are mastering the new? To what extent is the new in place now? Could it be institutionalized in the activity profile and the informal culture of the school? Which requirements of activity-based learning in science, now given in the particular school, foster repeated use? Are there remaining difficulties to be solved, and of what nature are they? Who is supporting and stabilizing the new?

Institutionalization. What was the flow of events after the mastery of the new started to grow? Which indicators show routinized activity-based learning on a continuing basis? What happened and what was decided so that, inside the school, the new practice was broadly shared, incorporated into the life of the school, anchored in the curriculum, and given the value of a core element of the school's pedagogy?

Overall Goals of the Project

The above research was intended to meet a variety of goals, most of which resulted in products reported in this book. The goals include the following:

1. Writing 15 stories about productive schools with successful cases of activity-based learning in science. Four illustrative cases—one from each of the four countries—are presented in chapters 4 through 7 of this book.

2. Conducting a cross-site analysis of the cases and evaluation of the findings in view of differences and similarities among the countries. Patterns and examples of activity-based learning as found in this analysis are presented in chapter 8.

3. Gaining from the cross-site analysis an *explanatory framework* about sustained school improvement. A report of these processes of change in school practice is presented in chapter 9.

4. Generating some practical guidelines for implementing activity-based science education on the basis of the results. These are presented in chapter 10.

Chapter 3

Contexts of Elementary Science in Four Nations

Many factors influence students' learning, including teachers, schools, family backgrounds, societal influences, and the students' own personalities. Much research has been directed at understanding the nature and degree of influence of such variables. Although a review of this research is beyond the scope of this book, it should be noted that all such variables are important and have a significant impact. Delving into this past research and relating it to the IMPACT research would demand collecting information on each student's socioeconomic status and family background, as well as information on the value placed on education within students' respective societies, the educational philosophies influencing each student's education, the various levels of financial support for education, and a variety of other factors.

Although such an extensive analysis could not be undertaken in our study, it is essential to provide some context for the case studies reported here in order to make them intelligible and provide some understanding of the differences that exist among cases.

At the same time, we should mention that IMPACT is not a comprehensive study; it focuses only on one aspect of education, namely, the sustained practice of activity-based learning in elementary science teaching. Even so, there are several variables that require specific attention, including: the educational background of the teachers; how schools fit into the broader political and administrative framework; the educational goals that apply; the locus of control over the curriculum; and some other characteristics of the school system.

Given this need for contextual information about an IMPACT school, a brief description will be provided for each of the countries (in alphabetical order): Germany, The Netherlands, Sweden, and the United States. Within each of these descriptions, attention will be given to both the national and local contexts, to general curriculum patterns and practices, and to teacher preparation. This contextual information will enrich the comparison of the countries. Particular attention will be given to similarities and differences in terms of administrative control, curriculum development and implementation, teacher background, and educational goals.

GERMANY

National context

Since its unification in 1990, Germany has consisted of 16 states (*Laender*) with 79.7 million inhabitants. The school systems of each state are quite similar, although each state has its own school law.* Each state has autonomy over its public schools, with authority to develop its own syllabi and time schedules, regulations for teacher recruitment, planning standards for setting up and maintaining a school, preservice teacher education and in-service education.

Most elementary schools in the 16 states are public. They start after Kindergarten and cover Grades 1 through 4, which encompass mostly 6- to 10-year-old children. Berlin and Brandenburg, 2 of the 16 states, extend elementary schooling from Grades 1 through 6, as is done in the majority of West European countries.

In 1991 almost 3.4 million children attended over 16,000 elementary schools, and by the turn of this century the figure is expected to be considerably higher. In 1989, 122,138 teachers were employed in the elementary sector (Klemm, Böttcher & Weegen, 1992, p. 88). (Statistics from other sources may appear higher due to the inclusion of teachers who teach in both lower secondary [*Hauptschule*] and elementary schools. Such statistics show a total of 232,800 teachers in 1991 [cf. *BMBW*, 1992, p. 108].) The ratio of pupils to teachers was 20:1 in 1989. The actual class size currently varies between 24 and 28, with a trend towards larger class sizes during the coming years. It should be noted that the current average class size has decreased from approximately 37 pupils per class in 1970 (Klemm et al., 1990, p. 86).

---

* The following description draws upon Riquarts (1988) and Bundesminister für Bildung und Wissenschaft (1989).

The IMPACT project focuses on the education of the 9- and 10-year-old children who are taught in Grades 3 and 4 of the elementary schools. Fig. 3.1 identifies the elementary school as the baseline for lower and upper secondary schools.

Before we describe the context of our cases, some remarks should be presented to illustrate the limited power of control from the national level. There are only limited areas of national educational policy-making, which are adjusted across the states. To some extent, the Standing Conference of Ministers of Education (KMK) is responsible for cross-state policy-planning. Recommendations of the KMK, however, are legally binding only if promulgated by state laws or decrees (Riquarts, 1988, p. 4). This decentralized system of policy and control is viewed as "cooperative federalism" (Baumert & Goldschmidt, 1980, p. 80). Since the statutes of the KMK require unanimity for their recommendation, once adopted they are virtually binding.

The Federal-State Commission for Educational Planning and Research Funding (BLK) is another institution serving the effort to promote initiatives for exploring school improvement in cases where the states share common concerns. The BLK was established in 1970. It contributes to school improvement by funding pilot school development projects, some of which are focused on elementary schools (see BLK, 1988; Meylan, 1983; Einsiedler & Ubbelohde, 1985). Elementary schools, however, cannot apply directly for money from BLK; they apply to state authorities.

Below the state level, the teacher of an elementary school can make use of in-service programs and counseling for school-based staff development. These services are offered by state-level institutes for teacher training and curriculum development. The demand for in-service courses depends on the teachers' individual choices. Some like to spend 6 or even 8 days a year if the principal can compensate the time in his or her school. The majority, however, attend only between 0 and 3 days a year. In the IMPACT schools, the use of in-service courses is a little above this average. Yet there is no formal obligation at all to participate in in-service training courses; most teachers are civil servants with full job security, and are not subject to rigorous sanctions. Retraining and further education depends upon the freedom of each individual.

On the regional and community levels, elementary teachers make increasing use of regional educational centers called *Lernwerkstatt*. The staff in a regional center consists predominantly of experienced teachers; the number of *Lernwerkstaetten* is currently growing, as is their popularity and acceptance. In the state of Schleswig-Holstein, in which one of our IMPACT schools is located, eight such centers currently serve the

FIGURE 3-1
Structure of the German School System

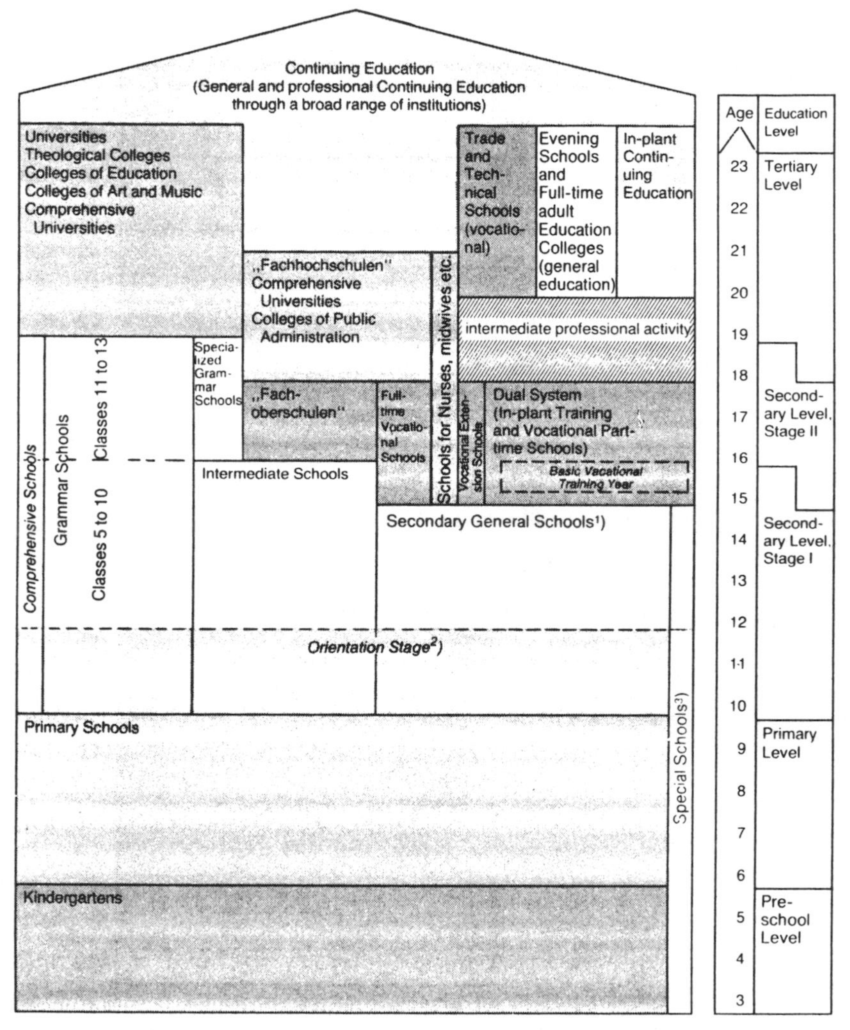

1) About 30 per cent of pupils in Secondary General Schools in addition attended an additional tenth school year.
2) About 73 per cent of pupils in the fifth an sixth school years attented the Orientation Stage.
3) There are also special schools at the intermediate, grammar and Vocational school levels.

- Diagramm of the basic structure of the education system in the Federal Republic of Germany: There are slight differences within the individual Laender.
- Figures in the right column show the earliest possible age of entry in an uninterrupted progress through the education system.
- The size of the rectangle is not proportional to the numbers attending.

school upon request. Teachers can learn about new curriculum materials, open education, how to utilize printing techniques in classroom work, and how to implement project methods, among other educational challenges for which on-site help is strongly needed.

The accessibility of a *Lernwerkstatt* plays a stimulating role in two IMPACT cases (Hamburg and Bremen). A *Lernwerkstatt* will be described briefly in chapter 5.

Local context

The following picture shows a typical elementary school setting. Although such situations vary among communities and states, the picture illustrates a typical contextual network of services, external support, and administrative links.

Each school has a principal elected by a committee consisting of members from the school, the community, and administrative authorities. The Ministry of Education is responsible for the instructional plan (*Lehrplan*) which consists of obligatory parts and many choices. A regional school authority (*Schulamt*) is responsible for inspecting and advising schools and for allocating personnel. The *Schulträger* is another agency, responsible for setting up school buildings, maintaining them, and providing money for equipment. The Schulträger is not responsible for paying for curriculum materials and other learning aids. Within each school is a "school conference" which varies in size according to the size of the school. Parents and children represent 50% of the school conference; the other half consists of teachers and the headmaster. The conference elects the chairman who may or may not be the headmaster.

An elementary school can turn for external assistance to the Institute for Science Education or other support agencies, depending on its needs. On the pre-service level, teachers are educated at a college of education, an institution which offers to varying degrees courses and other services. No formal relations exist between the college of education and an individual school.

The majority of elementary school teachers are members of the teachers' union. The union is rather powerful. It not only bargains for more personnel and more money for teachers, it also participates in setting up plans and proposals for school development.

In-service education and help for staff development are also provided through a state-level in-service training institute which has departments on the regional level as well. The in-service training institute is quite powerful, because the courses it offers define the support available.

FIGURE 3-2
Map of an Elementary School and its Immediate Contextual Network

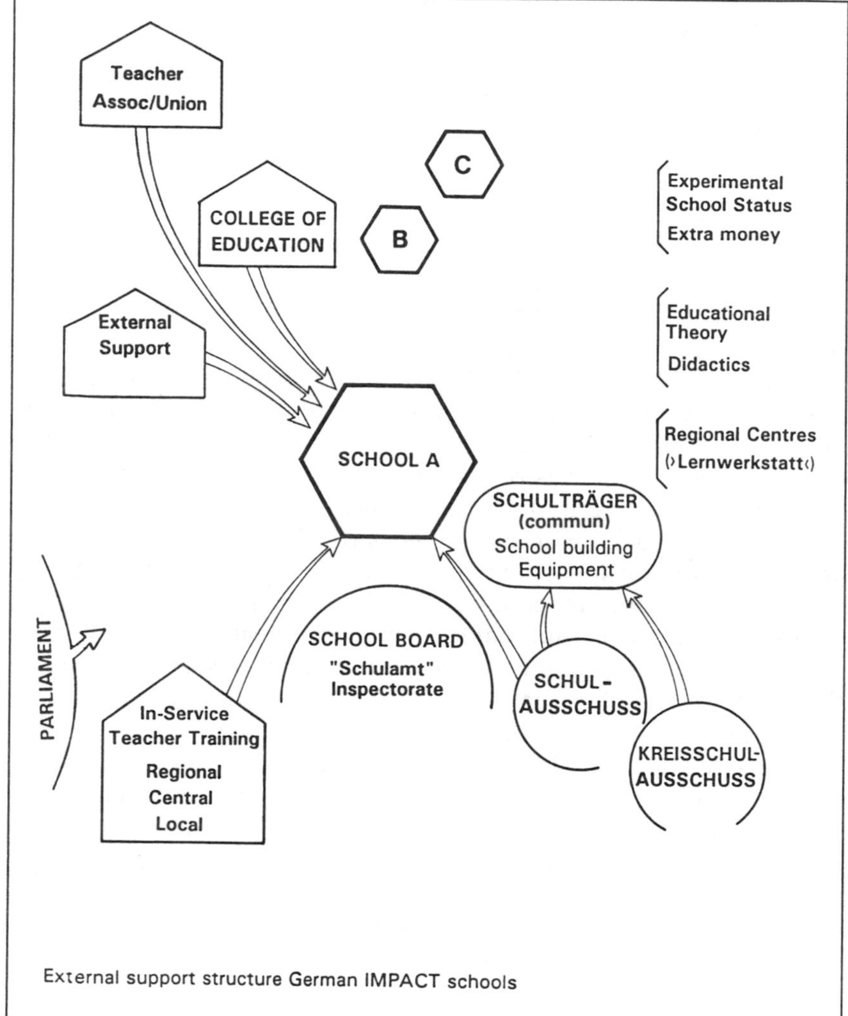

Curriculum and instructional framework

Nine- and 10-year-old children attend their schools for roughly 40 weeks per year. They have a 6-week summer holiday, an additional 2 weeks in autumn, 10 to 14 days over Christmas, and a 1- to 2-week holiday at Easter. The school week for a 9-year-old pupil covers up to 29 lessons—for a 10-year-old, 34 lessons—with each lesson lasting 45 minutes. Some of the lessons may be paired (*Blockstunde*) into 90-minute sessions.

Most elementary schools are not *Ganztagsschulen*: only 6% of the schools in the "old Laender" have full-day schedules. Schools normally start at 8:00 or 9:00 a.m. and finish at noon or 1:00 p.m. There are current discussions about extending the school day and blocking the time for school attendance in a manner that will enable parents who both work to pick up their children in a more reliable manner.

The 5- or 6-day elementary school week is divided up into 25 to 34 class periods (45 minutes each) of which general studies (*Sachunterricht*) cover between three and four periods per week. Only one-fifth of the week, often less, is actually devoted to science topics (Schreier, 1992), although the schools vary considerably in this regard. The choice of topics is partly within the autonomy of the individual teacher, although the syllabus provides a general orientation.

Parents, however, cannot decide to send their children to other schools, where a teacher may spend 50% of *Sachunterricht* on science issues. Elementary school enrollment is not competitive; parents can enroll their children only in the particular school that belongs to their residential area, or in the small number of private schools where rules of enrollment are different (e.g., Rudolf Steiner schools). Communities define which parts of the community belong to which school, with travel distances generally kept short. A child normally spends between 10 and 20 minutes to reach the school. The density of elementary school networks in urban or suburban areas is quite good.

Concerning the core curriculum, elementary schools are "to provide children with the basic knowledge required for further education while nurturing as much as possible the special abilities and interests of each individual child" (Secretariat of the Standing Conference of Ministers of Education and Cultural Affairs of the Laender, 1982, p. 15).

A timetable (*Stundenplan*) for the school is normally set up on a yearly basis and can be attuned to new requirements. The *Stundenplan* is divided into different subjects according to what is required in the syllabus (*Lehrplan*). A school can often identify one or two lessons which are not allocated in the above-mentioned subjects so that school-based options (*Verfuegungsstunde*) are possible. The classroom teacher can partially reschedule the time of the week for what is taught in class. For instance, a German lesson could be reallocated from Monday to Friday so that more space for another subject becomes available. If the

FIGURE 3-3
Typical Weekly Timetable in a German Elementary School

Schule

Stundenplan für 1991/92

Klasse: 4b   Klassenlehrer:

Zeit	Montag	Dienstag	Mittwoch	Donnerstag	Freitag	Sonnabend
$7^{40} - 8^{25}$	Deutsch	—	Sp / —	Deutsch	Deutsch	
$8^{30} - 9^{15}$	Mathemat.	Deutsch	Sp / Mus.	Mathemat.	Mathemat.	
$9^{25} - 10^{10}$	Schwimmen	Musik	Deutsch	Hei u. Sach U.	Kunsterz.	
$10^{25} - 11^{10}$	bis 10^{45} Elem	Mathemat.	Mathemat.	Werken	Religion	
$11^{20} - 12^{05}$	Hei. u. Sach. U.	Hei. u. Sach U.	Hei u. Sach U.			
$12^{15} - 13^{00}$	(Instrum)	Kunsterz.	(Chor)			
		Kl.				

Kiel, den 13.8.1991

D. Weiß
Klassenlehrer

[signature]
Rektor

classroom teacher teaches *Sachunterricht* and music, it is normally no problem to block these 2 hours so that an extended period of time is available for experiments or other activities.

Sachunterricht provides two to four lessons per week of introduction to Social Studies, History, Geography, Biology, Physics, and Chemistry. In addition, Mathematics, Religious Instruction, Music, Art, Sewing or Crafts, and Physical Education are obligatory in the curriculum, along with introductory reading and writing in the German language. The instructional time spent during a week varies between 20 and 30 hours.

The German IMPACT cases concentrate on activity-based learning in general studies (*Sachunterricht*) where varied use is made of the pupils' everyday life experiences. Science and technology issues are dealt with in this subject, with the aim of preparing pupils for learning about nature and how to inquire into natural phenomena, among other concerns. Links to life experiences get a growing emphasis in both theory and practice. The choice of topics and activities is, in many cases, open to the teacher's decision within the limits of the syllabus, which is somewhat loosely framed (Bernstein, 1971) as compared to the secondary curriculum. Additionally, elementary schools are encouraged to use instructional freedom for varied forms of open education (*geoeffneter Unterricht*; cf. Wallrabenstein, 1991; and examples in Hameyer, Lauterbach & Wiechmann, 1992).

A typical school day

More and more schools are reorganizing the breaks in their daily schedules. In some cases there is no school bell, so that the teachers can partially decide when to stop or start a lesson. In other cases, schools take at least one break that includes time for a common breakfast for the students; the breakfast is not provided by the school. During a break, students go outside to play soccer, run around, and engage in other informal play activities with their classmates; there is enough space at nearly all schools for such free-time activities.

Two examples of student schedules will illustrate more specifically how students spend their time.

Example A. The first example is from a school of 220 students, in which a 10-year-old boy named Tim is following a typical schedule for the school. He is starting the week with his classmates and the teacher in a morning circle discussion (*Morgenkreis*). They are given 25 minutes for talking about their experiences over the weekend. They have mastered shared rules of effective communication, so the teacher need not guide the discussion. During the *Morgenkreis*, they also discuss some ideas about what to do during the current week. After the discussion circle, Tim and his classmates set up their own individual week-plan. They are aware of the minimum requirements for this week and of the choices among which they may choose (cf. the example in chapter 5).

The *Morgenkreis* is followed by a learning period of 90 minutes, which starts with a reading exercise. The remaining 60 minutes are free for individualized work in the German language. The students often organize themselves into small groups; some prefer to learn alone when they work with individualized learning materials. Most of them know where to find which material. Tim does not need to be assisted by the teacher, who is advising others according to demand.

After this period, the big break of the day follows. After the break Tim attends *Sachunterricht* for the next 90 minutes, which is the place where students are taught science. He uses activity cards which contain ideas for hands-on activities or experiments he can conduct, preferably in cooperation with a classmate. Again, individual advice from the teacher is available upon request.

The environment of Tim's classroom offers various learning materials, including games, books, and simple equipment for constructive tasks. A printing machine is ready for free use, and a little learning studio where Tim likes to learn with his friend is only semi-separated from the classroom. Today his friend's mother is assisting the teacher with this lesson.

Example B. This school is located in a suburban section of a medium-sized city. Many children are living in one-parent families, and a large number of the children belong to families in which one of the parents works. In other cases, both parents have jobs, so they are out almost all day. Many of the pupils are looked after by outside help at home. Characteristic daily routines result.

Bernd, who attends third grade, is a good example of a student at this school. He gets up with his parents at 6:00 a.m. and his parents drive him to school at 7:40 a.m. Otherwise he stays alone at home, usually watching videos, until about 8:10 a.m. then walks or takes a city bus to school. At school he is very alert during the first periods, but as the morning goes on he becomes tired. He is interested in *Sachunterricht*. He has an enormous amount of previous knowledge from reading and watching television. He does not have enough stamina to work on a topic for a long period of time in spite of a lot of available materials and the possibility of working on his own.

FIGURE 3-4
Environment of an Open-Education Class

His homework is inadequate and probably done without enthusiasm. Bernd goes to a day nursery after school. Here he eats lunch and does his homework, together with 12 other children who attend three different schools and belong to five different grades. Social life in the group is very restless. When the weather is good they can play outside, but they are usually inside. Bernd's mother picks him up at about 4:00 p.m. His father returns home around 5:00 p.m.

Bernd usually spends 6 to 8 hours a day with other children. During this time there is no chance for him to be alone or to talk to someone about a problem. At home his mother has to do housework or go shopping. When Bernd does not have to help, he watches television or plays until dinner. Once a week he has sporting activities at 4:30 p.m.

The family regularly eats dinner at 6:00 p.m. Afterwards Bernd may watch television. He is seldom able to go fishing with his father. Bernd is usually allowed to watch television until 9:00 p.m., sometimes later. Only occasionally, he reads a book in the evening; he has a television and a computer in his room.

Brigitta, a fourth grader, is another student from this school. She has many interests and is encouraged at home. She gets up at 6:30 a.m. with her older brother (age 14). She has a 12 minute walk to school; on her way she picks up two girl friends who are in the same sports club. Brigitta is very popular in her class without being pushy and is very balanced.

Monday is currently her favorite day because she has three periods of swimming. After fifth period she voluntarily takes part in a music group that sings and plays instruments. After school she goes immediately home with her two girl friends and eats lunch with her family at 1:30 p.m. Following lunch she does her homework quickly and competently. In addition to playing with friends, she also has several other planned activities every week. Her favorite place is a nearby riding stable where she is allowed to ride once a week. She belongs to a gymnastics group in her sports club. Once a week she goes to recorder lessons with other children from her class. She usually watches an early evening program on television. After dinner she can either read or play. She goes to bed at 8:00 p.m., and has to have the lights out at 8:30 p.m. at the latest.

Teacher preparation

Pre-service teacher education is provided within universities and by institutions of higher education called *Paedagogische Hochschule*. Some states prepare teachers for teaching at a specific level of education (i.e., for the elementary level, the lower secondary level, *Hauptschule, Realschule Gymnasium*, Special Education, and others).

Only in a few cases is *Sachunterricht* a constituent part of the teacher-education curriculum. A prospective teacher normally studies two or three subjects according to the specific requirements of the state. Although *Sachunterricht* is usually taught by every teacher in an elementary school, it does not have any good equivalent in the teacher-education curriculum except at the in-service level.

Admission to teacher education depends on the final examination of the Gymnasium (*Abitur*), which is the end of secondary education at Grade 13. Teacher education comes in two stages, consisting of academic studies and on-the-job training. The teacher education curriculum consists of basic preparation in educational and social studies, the two or three subjects to be taught, and instructional planning. In most cases, a student in a *Paedagogische Hochschule* has to learn teaching during several *Praktika* of several weeks each. The amount of on-site practical experience is much smaller for student teachers from universities.

Within the states, there is ample opportunity for in-service teacher-education courses. Teachers can update knowledge and skills in the subjects they teach, as well as in educational psychology and didactics.

The German IMPACT schools

The German IMPACT schools are located in the northern part of Germany: two in Bremen and one each in Hamburg, Lower Saxony and Schleswig-Holstein.

THE NETHERLANDS

National context

The Netherlands is a Western European country of small geographic size but with a very high population density; the number of inhabitants is about 15 million. Some basic facts about the elementary education system include the following:

- elementary schools are meant for children from ages 4 through 12;
- there are about 8,400 elementary schools;
- these schools employ about 80,000 teachers;
- they serve a total of 1,400,000 students;
- most schools have between 100 and 200 students (170 on average);

- 70% of the schools are governed by private boards, and 30% by municipal boards;
- all schools receive public funding.

The educational system is both centralized (in general educational policy-making, formulation of standards, examination, and financial regulation) and decentralized (in terms of freedom to establish schools and in the autonomy of schools in curricular and instructional matters).

An elaborate system for school support services includes the following:

- 60 local and regional advisory centers (mean staff-size is about 40);
- 3 large national advisory centers;
- 42 teacher-education colleges (for pre- and in-service education);
- 3 separate national institutes for, respectively, curriculum development (SLO), test development (CITO), and the coordination of educational research (SVO).

Local context

The role of provinces or regions in educational matters is very weak in the Netherlands. The administration of schools is locally organized. The municipality has the authority over public education, and private foundations or associations (usually based on Catholic or Protestant denominations) have authority over private schools. Most of these boards govern only one or a few schools, so the administrative diversity is rather large. Also typical for the Dutch elementary education system is the relatively large number of small schools.

Each individual school has to describe the organization and content of their education in a "school work-plan." An elementary school offers education for 8 consecutive years, starting at the age of 4 (the first year not being obligatory). Thus, the target group of pupils in the IMPACT project (ages 9 and 10) is in its fifth and sixth years of schooling. A typical school week for these children has about 25 hours.

A typical school day

A typical school day for a 9- to 10-year-old student might be as follows: Every school day (Monday through Friday) the class starts at 8:30 a.m. The children usually live near the school building so they can walk or bicycle to the school in a few minutes.

The work in the morning continues until 11:45 a.m., with a break of 15 minutes halfway through. The teacher is responsible for all subjects, except music, which is taught by a special teacher.

Most pupils go home for lunch, but some will stay at the school, where some parents are usually responsible for supervision during that time. In the afternoons (except on Wednesdays) the children have school from 1:15 p.m. until 3:30 p.m.

Curriculum patterns and practices

The Elementary Education Act of 1985 gives an overview of subjects to be taught in every school. It mentions the domain of "natural sciences, including biology" as one of those subjects. Several studies in recent years have revealed that science has a very modest place in the curriculum practices of the "average" elementary school and classroom. Some more specific elements of this general picture are:

- There are large differences in science teaching, not only among but also within schools.
- Few schools establish priorities for the improvement of their science programs.
- Content is often restricted to biology topics.
- The average time spent on science is about 45 minutes, but there are large variations.
- The activity-based learning approach is seldom adequately realized; more passive forms of learning dominate.
- In the upper level (ages 8 through 12) biology textbooks without the spirit of activity-based learning dominate.
- External support for the improvement of science teaching is ineffective; few advisory centers have special expertise in the science domain.
- Pressure from society outside the school for the improvement of science is rather weak.

Although this is a somewhat disenchanting image of the current practice in science teaching, several initiatives for improvement can be mentioned. The most important effort stems from 1978, when the National Institute for Curriculum Development (SLO) initiated a large project for elementary science education (NOB). The main characteristics of the NOB project include: the integration of elements from various disciplines, such as biology, physics, and chemistry; an emphasis on active forms of learning (especially inquiry learning) and the stimulation of hands-on experience with concrete objects. The main goals of the NOB project are to broaden the subject matter domain to include most of the natural sciences and to promote an activity-based learning approach to science.

The NOB project was completed in 1991. Many curriculum documents and materials have been developed. Although the design and evaluation strategy involved the participation of several dozen schools, the impact of the project on the science practices of most other schools is still small. There are, however, some promising trends. A national document with a description of achievement goals for the different subject domains in elementary education has been published recently. Its section on science is very much in line with the curricular proposals of the NOB project. One may expect that it will encourage the cooperation of various stakeholders and stimulate their efforts to implement innovations in the science curriculum. This trend is clearly illustrated by the fact that several commercial publishers have taken the initiative to develop, promote, and distribute new science textbooks and materials that strongly reflect a NOB approach. It also seems that both a growing concern over the natural environment and proposals for a better technological orientation of pupils increase the pressure on the educational system to pay more attention to science-related topics.

Nevertheless, it is a realistic conclusion that at this moment the use of "modern" activity-based learning approaches in science within Dutch elementary schools is limited. In those schools where implementation efforts have already been made, individual teachers face many problems. The four most serious problems appear to be (cf. van den Akker, 1988):

1. The preparation of the science lessons is regarded as very complex and especially time-consuming.
2. Teachers experience a lack of subject matter knowledge and related skills, leading to low self-confidence.
3. Teachers find it difficult to change their teaching roles, especially with regard to a form of inquiry learning in which the emphasis is more on guidance of student activities than on presentation of knowledge.
4. Teachers express an unclear view of student learning outcomes.

Teacher preparation

The education of teachers for elementary schools is, at the moment, provided by 42 teacher-training colleges with a 4-year program. The majority (25) of these colleges are part of larger institutions for higher education; the remaining 17 colleges are more or less independent. A rather turbulent process of restructuring and retrenchment in recent years has caused many organizational, financial, and personnel problems for all colleges.

The formal program is very broad; graduates are expected to be capable of teaching all subjects, but many critics raise questions about the quality of their knowledge and skills. The actual programs, as practiced in the various colleges, differ widely in their attention to science education. The average time spent on science is estimated at about 150 hours, spread over 4 years. Although there is a tendency towards a more integrated approach (inspired by the NOB project), many programs still reflect a distinction between biology and physics. A frequently mentioned dilemma concerns the fact that the amount of time needed for adequate pedagogical training in inquiry skills is usually found at the expense of the desired breadth and depth of disciplinary knowledge. This problem is made even worse by the very limited science knowledge of most students entering the teacher-training institutes. Moreover, a suitable textbook for science education in teacher training is lacking. Some improvements in this unfavorable situation are anticipated from recently published curriculum materials offering a wide array of practical suggestions for lessons that are frequently used in teacher training.

The influence of in-service education in science at the moment is still rather small. Despite some promising local initiatives, few schools show active interest, and the organization of in-service activities is often rather inefficient.

The Dutch IMPACT schools

Not surprisingly, in view of this general situation in elementary science education, it is hard to find Dutch schools with a successful history of activity-based learning approaches in science. An especially restrictive criterion in the selection of the IMPACT schools is that such an approach should not be the exclusive style of one or two highly gifted and motivated teachers, but preferably that of the majority of the teaching staff.

As a general pattern, two sorts of "success" schools can be distinguished. The first category concerns a group of 24 schools that have been involved in the evaluation of the NOB project. These schools were asked to use the developed curriculum for a 2-year period (1986-88). The developers hoped to receive feedback about material and curricular revisions and also to explore what kind of support schools need to further the implementation process. Besides the materials, the schools received some support, mainly through an introductory conference and several site visits by a NOB developer in the first year.

The second category of potentially successful schools includes the elementary schools (from 5% to 10% of the total) that have historical roots in the tradition of certain pedagogical movements inspired by such founders as Montessori, Freinet, and Petersen. It is a common characteristic of these schools that they attach great value to activity-based learning. That preference is not exclusive to the science domain, but is a feature across the curriculum. Whereas for most Dutch schools activity-based learning in science is a twofold innovation, one might say that for these schools it is more or less an extension or sharpening of their pedagogical tradition to the science domain.

SWEDEN

National context

Sweden is a country with a rather large geographic area and a total of approximately 8 million inhabitants. All the Swedish schools in the IMPACT study are part of the *grund*-school system, which enrolls about 98% of the students. The remaining 2% of the school children belong to "free schools" that are also publicly financed. The IMPACT research has focused on the education given to 9- and 10-year-old students; in Swedish schools, these students are in their third and fourth years of schooling.

The basic organizational unit of the *grund*-school is the school-management area (*rektorsomrade*). Within such school-management areas, one usually finds about 600 to 800 students, about 70 to 80 teachers, 2 to 3 school leaders, and about 30 people working with food services, student care, counseling, maintenance services, clerical tasks, etc. Within each school-management area, there are about 3 or 4 school sites. In larger cities, however, a school-management area may have only one site; while in rural and sparsely populated areas of Sweden, one may find as many as 12 to 15 smaller schools within the school-management area.

The school-management area is an administrative part of the geographical area of a *kommun*. Sweden is divided into 286 *kommuns*. The largest *kommun* is Stockholm with its 800,000 inhabitants while the smallest one, Sorsele, has only about 4,000 inhabitants. Most of the *kommuns* have between 10,000 and 40,000 inhabitants. Ninety of the *kommuns*, however, have less than 10,000 inhabitants and most of them cover huge geographical areas. Each *kommun* has its local parliament that reflects local political opinions. In each *kommun*, there are different local political boards focused on important tasks like finances, social welfare, culture, environmental questions, leisure-time activities, and schools. The members of the local board of schools of the *kommun* are elected for three-year periods as representatives of various political parties. The local board that deals with education usually appoints a managing director of the school system of the *kommun* and usually (if the *kommun* is large enough) this director has an office that works with both economic and pedagogical issues in relation to the schools of the *kommun*. All *grund*-schools in Sweden are publicly financed. The *grund*-school is in many ways a centralized school system, as the state decides on a national curriculum and the allocation of time to different school subjects. The *kommuns* are autonomous, however, in many areas, such as how to organize the work, the buildings, maintenance services, transportation, student food services, and the learning materials of the students. All these areas of the school may differ among the *kommuns*, as may the local working plans among the different school-management areas. The *kommun* also appoints school leaders and teachers and pays their salaries.

Local context

The Swedish school-management area usually has an inner structure which is divided into several working units for each school. These working units are usually composed of between two and four classes. Within the school's working units, the teachers are expected to cooperate in the planning of the educational process and money distribution, as well as give instruction to the students and manage their work together. In each working unit, one of the teachers is appointed as the "study leader." When appointed as a study leader, the teacher's teaching responsibility is reduced by a few hours per week to allow the teacher to act in this capacity. Ideally, this study leader will take the initiative to improve the quality of teaching in the unit. The study leader is also expected to be active in planning the in-service training of the team and respond to the leader of the school-management area about the way in which the unit plans, deals with its money, and evaluates its own work.

In most school-management areas, the school leader and his or her deputies use these teachers as "sub-managers" in the school-management process. The school leader, deputies and study leaders meet regularly to decide on such important local topics as how the local working plan is to be developed, in what way the in-service training of the teachers is to be organized during the year, and what money to budget for the next year. Since the local organization—the school-management area—is based on geographical limits, the school leaders are not always found at the local school site. His or her office may be in a distant building somewhere else within the school-management area.

General curriculum patterns and practices

The Swedish *grund*-school contains nine grades. During the first three grades—the lower stage—the students have one main teacher. This teacher may be assisted in some cases by a special teacher whose task it is to help students with learning disabilities. During the first 3 years, the students in these grades spend 16, 17, and 20 hours per week, respectively, in school dealing with schoolwork. In Grade 3, the students spend a total of about 30 hours per week at school. The 10 hours not spent on schoolwork are used for eating and playing with others.

During the next 3 school years—Grades 4, 5, and 6, called the "middle stage"—another teacher is mainly responsible for the education of the students. As the students now spend about 23 hours per week at schoolwork, more teachers enter the scene. In addition to the class teacher, there is a special teacher working with tasks similar to those in the lower stage. The students now also meet some subject specialists, such as teachers working with handicrafts or physical education, although the latter teacher is not found in all schools with middle stage students. During the lower and middle stages of the *grund*-school, the students are organized in classes that cannot be larger than 25 students; the average class contains about 22 to 23 students. The students in the Swedish school described in the IMPACT project belong to the lower stage, Grade 3, and the middle stage, Grade 4.

During the final 3 years of the *grund*-school, the classes are slightly larger and the students meet subject specialists who follow them during the last 3 years of their *grund*-school education. Two of these subject teachers have a special responsibility towards the class: they are appointed as *klassforestandare*, which means they are responsible for the students of the class and their social life at the school. They are also key persons in relation to parents and act as spokespersons for the students in many meetings with teachers. The students now spend about 24 hours per week on schoolwork. The curriculum of the *grund*-school of Sweden, the *laroplan*, is decided on by Parliament and by the government. In the *laroplan*, the use of time for different subjects is regulated. The 166 pages of the *laroplan* are divided into three main sections. In the first section, the main aims of the school are explained, along with a presentation of some guidelines as to how one may reach these aims through schoolwork. Among other things, there are recommendations in this part of the *laroplan* about the ways in which students and teachers are expected to work to stimulate the best student social development. In the second section, the aims of the different subjects are defined and described. The last section describes the distribution of time among different subjects during the school year.

Since the beginning of the 1980's, each local organizational unit of the *grund*-school system in Sweden has also been requested to produce a fourth part to its curriculum—a local working plan—that should be based on the *laroplan*, but contain what the local organization wants to emphasize.

In Sweden, the school week for 9-year-old students consists of 30 lessons, and for 10-year-old students, 34 lessons, with a lesson being 40 minutes long. The week is divided into various subjects including: Swedish, music, mathematics, handicrafts, sports, different "orientering" subjects such as geography, history, civics, and science, as well as English, which starts at age 9. At age 9 the student spends 18 lessons per week on orientering subjects, with the amount of this time devoted to science being decided by the student and the teacher. Ten-year-old students spend 21 lessons per week on orientering subjects, with at least 6 of them devoted to natural science. More weekly time can be spent on natural science if the teacher and student so decide.

A typical school day

The homes of most Swedish students living in cities are quite close to their schools so they do not have to travel a long way. Usually they walk or bike to the school if close enough, but some students have to go by bus, taxi or sometimes even by boat or ferry, since some regions are sparsely populated. Therefore, some students have to travel for 30 minutes to an hour to reach school. At 10 minutes after 8:00 the work starts.

The first working period of the day lasts until 9:40 a.m. During the first 80 minutes of the day the work may be concentrated on Swedish. Between 9:40 a.m. and 10:00 a.m. there is a break during which students play outside the school building. Most school sites have a lot of space in which to play and usually there are natural settings for those who want to go into them. During the break, students may play soccer or jump rope, or if it is winter, throw snowballs.

Between 10:00 a.m. and 11:20 a.m., the students work again. Now it may be time to spend 40 minutes on music, and after that, 40 minutes on history. At 11:20 a.m. they walk to the school cafeteria for a warm meal, including bread and butter and a glass of milk.

After lunch, the remainder of the time until 12:10 p.m. is spent outdoors. Between 12:10 p.m. and 1:10 p.m. students work with handicraft or wood, followed by a 10 minute break. The last part of the day, from 1:20 p.m. until 2:40 p.m., is shared between studies in English and math. By about 3:00 p.m., students who live near the school will be home.

Teacher preparation

Teacher education is a part of the university system in Sweden. Students are selected for teacher education on the basis of the grades received in their last class of secondary school. They spend between 3 ½ and 4 ½ years at the teacher college at the university before being permitted to take a job as a teacher. Preparation of the new teachers covers a broad range of subjects, including science. Knowledge of different school subjects is treated, as well as knowledge in the fields of pedagogy and teaching methodology. Courses on child and youth development, as well as courses on education as a cultural and societal phenomenon, are compulsory. Teachers are not only prepared to educate children in subjects with a strong cognitive load, but also in subjects that have a more physical or emotional focus such as music, art, and sports.

Critical voices are raised now and then in Sweden saying that too little activity-based learning is used in the education of teachers; their education is perceived as too traditional. There are also critical voices that say teachers are too narrowly educated and that the widened role of teachers is treated inadequately. By this the critics mean that teachers deal too little with such broad educational matters as how you can help students from immigrant families, and different living conditions of Swedish children and youth. The critical voices also claim that the education of teachers contains too much of ordinary school practice and does not develop independent behavior among beginning teachers.

The Swedish IMPACT cases

In Sweden, all elementary schools where 9- to 10-year-olds are taught ought to have institutionalized the activity-based learning pattern. The Swedish *läroplan*—the central guidelines that all schools in the country are expected to follow—prescribes that schools shall use this kind of working pattern among other working methods. Investigations of the use of different working patterns in Sweden (SÖ, 1990), made during the same period that IMPACT schools were being selected, show that regular use of activity-based learning principles is not a common practice. Even so, since the pressures on schools to use this kind of working pattern have existed for many years in Swedish society, some schools were found in which a large group of teachers really practiced these principles.

The three schools that were selected for the study are in three different locations. One school, where activity-based learning has been practiced for the past 6 years, is situated in a suburb of the second largest city in Sweden (with half a million inhabitants). Here the staff was selected to work in a newly built school where activity-based learning was proclaimed in advance to be an important part of school life. Another school was found in a small town situated on a large island in the middle of the Baltic Sea. The third school is in a small industrialized village in the midst of a farming district in southern Sweden. In the latter two schools, the teachers started using activity-based learning as they became interested in it and sought a change in teaching methods. In one of these two schools, activity-based learning principles have been in use for the past 7 to 8 years, in the other for the past 14 years.

The United States

National context

The United States of America is large in geographic area and has a population of approximately 260 million people. It is a very diverse country in terms of climate and land forms, as well as in the ethnic mix of its people and the location of its people in both dense urban settings and sparsely populated rural areas. The country consists of 50 states, each with a substantial amount of autonomy with respect to some matters, one of which is education.

Because of significant differences between the role of the national government in educational matters in the United States and that typically found in most other countries in the world, it is important to describe the nature of the federal government's role in the education of students in the United States. The role of the federal government in the education of elementary and secondary school students is relatively small. The constitution of the country specifically assigns responsibility for education to the individual states. Curriculum, staffing and financing of schools is a state matter, with each of the 50 states having the freedom largely to define education as it wishes. On the average in the United States, only 7% of the money spent on the education of a student comes from the federal budget; the remaining 93% comes from state and local school district appropriations. Almost all of the federal money is given to local school districts in support of special programs for which there is a national concern. These include "at risk students," handicapped students, and others for whom at some point in time an urgent need was perceived and the federal government initiated funding which in many cases has persisted through subsequent history.

State context

The 50 states have chosen to exercise their responsibility for education in a variety of ways; in some states a large number of curricular and other educational decisions are made at the state level, while in other states such decisions may be largely delegated to individual school districts.

For example, Colorado (where several of our case studies are located) is clearly at the decentralized end of this continuum. The state constitution says that curricular matters are the province of local school districts. While the beginnings of a state-wide testing program point to the potential erosion of some of this local control, decisions are clearly in the hands of local school district personnel. The type of science program to be used and the amount of time devoted to it during the school day are local decisions.

While a substantial portion of the budgets of local school districts comes from state appropriations of funds acquired through state sales taxes and state income taxes, these funds are largely dispensed on the basis of a formula that is independent of curricular matters. Local school districts have considerable freedom.

Essentially all of the states (Hawaii is the only exception) are divided into a number of districts (177 in the case of Colorado, for example) which are responsible for educational matters pertaining to students up to the age of approximately 18. Each such district has a policy-making board, which in almost all cases is selected by direct election of all of the people of voting age in the district. Candidates run without affiliation with any political party, and campaign issues are typically matters of local concern, not the least of which is the level of financial support for the schools. In addition to state appropriations, school districts receive money from local property taxes. Since the local board of education sets the rate of taxation (within parameters established by the state government) issues of taxation as well as educational policy come to the fore.

A typical school district has within it a number of individual schools. Usually there is a person known as the "superintendent" who is the chief administrative officer of the school district and who is directly answerable to the elected board of education, which has the power to hire and fire this person at will. Depending upon the size of the school district, the superintendent may have a central staff of none or many personnel to support the work of the school district. Each individual school within a school district has a principal as its chief administrative officer. Except in the case of an unusually small school, this person typically has no teaching responsibilities.

General curriculum patterns and practices

In the post-Sputnik era of concern about educational quality in the United States, several activity-based science curriculum development programs were initiated through federal funding from the National Science Foundation. These programs of the early 1960s yielded several versions of hands-on elementary school science programs which were then available for school adoption. It is important to note that there was no federal mandate that such programs be used. The federal government's role was simply that of providing funding for the development of several such programs. During the 1960s and on into the early 1970s, however, some federal money was allocated for in-service education of teachers and for other means of supporting the introduction of such new programs.

During that era a large number of schools in the United States chose to initiate one of these programs. They were widely regarded as superior to the existing programs; they represented a shift from textbook learning to hands-on science. One of the striking phenomena of this era was the large number of schools which initiated one of these programs and within a few short years drifted back to the former mode of instruction. This phenomenon, of course, is one of the prime motivators for conducting this case study and the other aspects of the IMPACT project.

Finally, an understanding of the highly decentralized educational approach in the United States requires mention of the rather high degree of uniformity across the many states. Both curriculum materials and approaches to teaching are far more similar than one may suspect given the country's decentralized approach. Among the factors which may lead to this uniformity is the easy movement of teachers from one part of the country to another. Hiring is done by local school districts and, by and large, a teacher prepared in a teacher-education institution anywhere in the country is qualified to take a position in any state. In addition, the curriculum materials, such as textbook series, are produced mostly by large publishing companies which market their materials nationally. Easy and widespread communication of many kinds among school personnel has resulted in a rather similar curricular pattern in schools across the country.

A typical school day

The established daily schedule within a school varies from one school to another in the United States, even within a local school system that has fairly centralized control over its schools. Even so, the typical school day looks fairly similar in schools across the country. The following schedule information is for the fourth grade in one of the schools involved in our case studies—Perris Elementary School. It resembles what would be found in other schools.

Students begin each day, Monday through Friday, at 8:00 a.m. They work primarily with one teacher in a self-contained classroom situation during the 6 1/2 hour school day. The classroom teacher is responsible for instruction in language arts, reading, math, social studies, and science. Special-area teachers work with the students in music, physical education, and art. The major academic emphasis in the fourth grade is on reading. The students in this school are grouped by ability into three reading groups; each group meets with the teacher for approximately 30 minutes per day. Math class meets for 55 minutes per day, while language arts instruction (spelling, writing, grammar, and speaking) occurs for about 45 minutes per day. Social studies and science are rotated; a unit in one of the subjects is taught, followed by a unit in the other subject area. One hour per day is allocated for science and social studies. The students have an opportunity to read self-selected materials for 15 minutes per day. This silent reading follows a 40 minute lunch and recess. Instruction in art, physical education, and music is provided by the special teachers who come in on a rotating schedule. The students go to the library weekly for 30 minutes to check out books and learn library research skills. They also work in the computer lab for 30 minutes per week. The school day concludes at 2:25 p.m.

8:00 a.m.	School Day Begins
8:05-8:50	Language Arts and Reading I
8:55-9:40	Special Classes (Art, Music and Physical Education)
9:45-10:00	Recess
10:00-10:30	Reading II (except: Wed., Computer Lab; Thur., Library)

10:30-11:00	Reading III
11:00-11:55	Mathematics
11:55-12:35 p.m.	Lunch and Recess
12:35-12:50	Silent Reading
12:50-1:50	Science or Social Studies
1:50-2:25	Language Arts
2:25 p.m.	Dismissal

Teacher preparation

As in the case of curriculum, there is far more uniformity in the preparation of teachers than one might expect, given that each state sets its own standards for the certification of teachers. (In contrast to the state certification of teachers, the employment of teachers, and such matters as salary, are a local district matter.) Because of such influences as the standards established by national professional associations, the certification standards among the states are similar enough that a teacher who has completed an approved teacher education program in one state can be employed in almost any other state with relative ease.

The typical elementary teacher has completed a 4-year bachelor's degree program designed for prospective elementary-school teachers. As with other U.S. college programs, about 2 years of the 4 required for the bachelor's degree is devoted to broad liberal arts study. Although some elementary education programs provide the student with a major in an academic field, most students in such programs acquire breadth rather than depth of subject-matter background. The specific science background of American elementary school teachers is minimal—essentially that required within the general liberal arts component of their bachelor's degree program. The average is two or three courses in the natural sciences (i.e., the equivalent of about a half-semester of study). Professional studies, including student teaching, constitutes the equivalent of approximately 2 or 3 of the 8 semesters in the majority of students' programs. Of this professional training, the typical teacher's program includes one course on the teaching of science. This course probably includes some training on how to teach hands-on science, although quite often it is a relatively minimal amount.

The American IMPACT schools

The four American cases (Anderson & Hower, 1994a; Anderson & Hower, 1994b; Mitchener, 1994; Muscella, 1994) were all school-district cases, although in each case one or two schools were selected from within the district for intensive study. Districts were selected because, in most instances where an entire school in the United States has an ongoing activity-based science program, it is the result of a district-level endeavor for initiating and sustaining such a program. Because one or two schools were selected for intensive study within each district, each one of the cases from the United States is in some sense both a case study of a district and of a school.

Three of the cases were located within the state of Colorado, although the activity-based science programs in these three districts developed entirely independently of each other. Colorado is on the local-control end of the U.S. continuum of local vs. state control, and none of these programs emerged as the result of state influence or initiative. The fourth case was located in a suburb of the greater Chicago, Illinois area. Another site for an IMPACT case study was sought within a different large metropolitan area (including numerous school districts and a population of about 1.5 million people) near the geographic center of the country, but a site that met the IMPACT selection criteria could not be found. This gives a hint as to how uncommon such activity-based science programs are among other types of schools in the U.S.

Of additional interest in the United States is the recent attention to the theoretical underpinnings of science education programs, as well as to practical bases for initiating the desired programs. In the late 1980s, the American Association for the Advancement of Science (AAAS) initiated its Project 2061, which resulted in the publication of *Science for All Americans* (Rutherford & Ahlgren, 1990). This project gave extensive attention to relating science to connected areas such as mathematics; focusing on the major themes of science; and attending to the interface of science and technology. With its attention to the foundations of learning and teaching, it is developing alternative curriculum models for the desired form of science education. An even more recent endeavor in the United States that encompasses elementary school science education is the National Science Education Standards Project housed at the National Research Council. Building on various other activities, such as Project 2061, a definition of desired practice is emerging, along with means of assessment. In each of these cases, the work is recent enough that it did not have an impact on the programs included in our case studies. These emerging forces are mentioned here, however, because they are potentially strong and because their outlook is largely consistent with the type of programs we selected for study in the IMPACT project.

Chapter 4

A Dutch Case: Regenboog

This school, Regenboog (pseudonym), belongs to a group of 24 "follow-up schools" of the NOB project. NOB is a large project for elementary science education initiated by the National Institute for Curriculum Development (SLO; for further details see chapter 3). These 24 schools were to use the NOB materials, which had been developed in cooperation with other schools, and to provide the developers with feedback based on their experiences.

The follow-up phase took 2 years (1986-88). At both the beginning and the end of this phase, two evaluation studies were conducted. Both studies had two components: a questionnaire survey for all teachers (n=175) in the participating schools, and written tests for the students (n=425) in the oldest group (age 12).

Regenboog was selected as a school for an IMPACT case study for two reasons. First, several informants recommended the school as being relatively successful in implementing the NOB approach. Second, it was the largest of the follow-up schools; the case description of this large school along with that of a small school in the group (see the report with the compilation of cases, Ekholm et al. 1994) might offer some insight into the influence of school size on the implementation of activity-based learning in science.

Data Collection

The methods of data collection included the following:

- a long semi-structured entry interview with the principal;
- several shorter and more informal follow-up conversations with the principal;

• a semi-structured entry group interview with three selected teachers of classes with 9- to 10-year-old students;

• observations of lessons given by each of these three teachers, immediately followed by individual interviews;

• a talk with a staff member of the local center for environmental education, conducted while the IMPACT researcher was there to observe a class which visited that center;

• interviews with two members of the NOB development team (one of them had been primarily responsible for the support of the school);

• the gathering of various documents and materials, such as the general information brochure of the school, the science part of the school workplan, print lesson-materials of teachers and worksheets of students who participated in the observed lessons.

Besides these new data, the questionnaire data mentioned earlier, collected from the teachers and the eldest group of students, were accessible.

School Characteristics

By Dutch standards, the Regenboog school is very large: it has about 600 students, 20 classes and 27 teachers (20 full-time and 7 part-time). It was the largest one in the group of follow-up schools and belongs to the 10 largest primary schools in the country. The 20 classes are divided into more than eight different age groups,* with a mean size of 30 students. Concerning students of the age targeted in the IMPACT case studies, there are two large classes of 9- to 10-year-old students of about 35 each, and three classes of 10- to 11-year-old students of about 25 each.

The Regenboog school has a large central building and five small additional sections. It is located in a rather new part of a mid-size town. The school was established in 1976 and has a Protestant identity. In its immediate surroundings there are also public and Catholic schools.

Of all teachers, 60% are female and 40% male. The principal is male and completely free of teaching tasks; the female assistant-principal is partly released from teaching. The composition of the teaching staff is rather stable; 90% of the teachers present at the start of the NOB period in 1986 were still present in 1989. The average amount of teaching experience is 13 years. Most teachers (70%) are between 30 and 40 years old.

---

*The Dutch elementary school covers eight grades, including Kindergarten, starting at the age of 4 years up to age 12. (For further detail see chapter 3 on educational context.)

One-third of the teachers have some specific background in science education from their pre-service training.

The whole teaching staff meets once a week. Moreover, every other week smaller meetings are held in three different sections, based on grade levels.

ACTIVITY-BASED LEARNING IN PRACTICE

The science curriculum

In the Spring of 1988 the Regenboog school produced a voluminous chapter of 30 pages about science education for its school work-plan. The publication of this document marked the transition from an exploratory period (since the summer of 1986) to a stage of stabilization and institutionalization for the entire team of teachers. A short overview of the contents of the document follows:

- preface (1 page);
- definition of science education (1 page);
- general aims and objectives (2 pages);
- description of aims and objectives for the different age groups (11 pages);
- general content structure (2 pages);
- program description for each of the eight age groups with specification of lesson themes and time allocation (8 pages) (About two-thirds of the year's program is fixed; the remaining time is available for topical matters and personal preferences. An illustrative selection of topic labels for the 9- to 10-year-old students includes: Differences between People; Chickens; Soil Animals; Insects and Flowers; Growth and the Growth of Life; Floating; Evaporation; Sounds and their Sources; Clouds; Ears; Eyes; Taste; Birds in the Winter; Batteries and Bulbs; Trees and Leafs; Weather Reports; Outdoor Excursions.);
- description of instructional strategies (3 pages);
- relation of science to other subject domains (2 pages).

The current document, written by the principal, draws strongly upon the NOB curriculum proposals. It is the school's intention to adapt the text to its own situation gradually over the next few years as more experience is gained.

General pattern of science teaching

The following summarizing information about the general pattern of science teaching in the school is based largely on teachers' responses to questionnaires.

• The average time spent on science is about 1 hour per week (with little variation among the teachers).

• The average time spent on lesson preparation is about 30 minutes per hour of teaching (with large variation among the teachers).

• The ranked order of distribution of the average time that teachers spend on different content areas (as distinguished by NOB) within the domain of science is: (1) human body, (2) animals, (3) plants, (4) environment, (5) weather and seasons, (6) materials and objects, and (7) technology.

• The most frequent teaching-learning activities are: (1) class conversations/discussions, (2) experiments in groups, (3) other group activities (e.g., observation, construction tasks). Individual activities are less frequent.

• The teachers use a wide range of resources; only one-third sometimes use a textbook or package from commercial publishers.

• The problems most frequently mentioned by the teachers are: an unclear view of student outcomes (82%); too much time needed for lesson preparation (70%); complex teaching roles (dealing with unexpected situations, helping individual students, maintaining goal-directedness) (67%); lack of subject matter knowledge (especially in physical and technological topics) (61%).

Perceptions of practice

During this study, observations were made of lessons in three different classes:

• a lesson of 1 hour about the theme "Heartbeat and Respiration" for a group of 33 students (ages 9 and 10);

• the same sort of lesson in a parallel class (34 students);

• a 2-hour excursion to the local center for environmental education with a class of 25 students (ages 10 and 11); the children received instruction and did group activities on the theme "Propagation of Humans, Plants, and Animals"

These observations provided vivid impressions of the practice of teaching and learning in classes within the IMPACT target group (ages 9 and 10). Moreover, they offered a fruitful basis for in-depth interviews with the teachers about their teaching practice, their experiences in recent years and their perception of the implementation of NOB in the school.

The following summary of impressions of the current science practice in the school is based on these observations and interviews, as well as on the interviews with the principal and with the NOB developer.

• The students are highly motivated for science activities; they think it is great fun. The children are usually very actively engaged in an enthusiastic atmosphere.

• The teachers report major changes in their teaching roles. Whole-class lecturing has sharply diminished, and more emphasis is put on student initiative and discovery activities, especially in group settings.

• The teachers also report significant changes in their beliefs and perceptions. Their attention to natural studies has strongly increased. They now regard NOB as an important and integrated part of their curriculum. These changes in their value system were nicely illustrated by the statement of one of the teachers that a "bad" (unsuccessful) NOB lesson is still better than the former biology lessons: "The children learn more from it. The hands-on activities with concrete objects and materials are essential for stimulating their minds and for eliciting curiousity." There is a common agreement among the teachers that activity-based science learning is both attractive and instructive for the children.

• The cooperation between teachers within grade levels is very intensive. They prepare their lessons together and exchange their experiences afterwards. The teachers emphasize that this mutual support has been extremely helpful and encouraging. Their firm belief is that without it, the implementation would have been much more difficult.

• The patterns of cooperation are not restricted to grade-level teachers. The teaching staff and several subgroups meet regularly for consultation. In general, the school has an open culture with much mutual feedback, common planning and decision making, and social support.

• These experiences and processes have led to a strong commitment to the NOB approach by the entire staff. There is no obstruction by opponents, and attempts to evade the new efforts seem to be lacking.

• The school wishes to increase its "ownership" of the NOB approach by gradually making more adaptations to their own situation and preferences, based on continued experience.

• It is obvious that the school principal plays a very important role in the implementation process. He has a great personal interest in natural studies and he is a declared supporter of the NOB approach. He fills several useful roles: internal consultant and trouble shooter, facilitator and coordinator, visionary and author.

Some teacher problems

Although the description above makes clear that considerable progress has been made with the implementation of activity-based learning in science, there are also problems to be mentioned. The observations, and particularly the interviews, reveal several problems that confirm and clarify most of the teaching problems that came up in the questionnaire survey. Most of the problems are focused on the instructional practice of individual teachers.

• The major and most persistent problem the teachers face concerns the large amount of time needed for solid lesson preparation; the time for lesson execution is also often perceived as too long. The teachers hope that more routinization will help, but they are a bit worried about the slow progress in this respect.

• Another occasional problem is related to the perception of teachers that their own science knowledge is insufficient. As a result, for certain lesson themes they feel obliged to complete an extensive subject orientation themselves. A lack of adequate background knowledge sometimes discourages them from starting with unfamiliar topics.

• During lessons, the teachers sometimes find it difficult to cope with the many ideas and initiatives that the children come up with. They often see no opportunity to deal with many interesting and worthwhile aspects of these initiatives. Sometimes they try to handle this problem by addressing such aspects in other subjects (e.g., by using the phenomenon of the annual rings of trees in math lessons).

• The teachers sometimes observe that the introduction of a new theme in a lesson takes too much time. As a consequence, too little time is left in the final stage of the lesson for evaluation of the discovery activities and for summing up the conclusions. Also, the time for reflection on the inquiry approach of the students tends to be small.

• The teachers sometimes find it hard to get a proper balance between the autonomous discovery work of the students and the amount and timing of teacher intervention for stimulation and structuring of the learning process.

• The teachers sometimes fear "organized chaos" in their classrooms, especially when many small groups work at different tasks at the same moment. They experience the activity-based learning approach in science as very demanding in large classes.

History of Activity-Based Learning

The history of activity-based learning in the school can be summarized in a brief sketch. Before 1986 there was a large variation within the school with respect to science education. Many teachers regarded it as a marginal subject domain. No collaborative team efforts were undertaken for improving science teaching. A few individual teachers (including the principal) were personally interested in nature studies, especially in biological themes. Some teachers made intensive use of the services of the local center for environmental education (excursions, lesson materials, etc.). Several other teachers, however, were not interested in biological or science issues at all. Probably the most accurate conclusion is that the majority of the teachers had a more or less neutral attitude toward science.

Initiation

In the Spring of 1986, a letter of invitation by the NOB project arrived. The school was requested to participate for a 2-year period as a follow-up school of the NOB project. The entire teaching staff decided in a plenary session to accept the invitation. The main arguments were:

- satisfaction about the state of affairs in other subjects;
- recognition that the approach to biology had been too one-sided;
- the opinion that their own program was rather unstructured.

It was crucial that the principal was very strongly in favor of participation. He perceived the program and presented it as a good opportunity to become oriented to and to practice "modern" teaching strategies.

The activities started with the participation of all teachers at an initial conference—with 11 other schools—organized by the NOB project. It was a 3-day conference that included: a general introduction; video-demonstrations of an activity-based learning approach to science; distribution of NOB lesson materials; ample time for exercises with the materials (direct experience with science activities); discussions; and planning. During the same period, a member of the NOB team visited the school for an introductory session on-site. These two activities provided the teaching staff with a clear and stimulating introduction for their participation in the project.

Implementation

In the 1986-87 school year, the NOB materials were used intensively, following the guidelines of a global year-plan. There was no compulsion—but much social pressure—to engage in the science activities. The permanent liaison officer of the NOB project paid regular visits to the school, usually 1 day each month. He frequently worked with small groups of teachers from each grade level, observing lessons and having talks with the teachers. Teaching-staff meetings concerning the project were also held reqularly, usually led by the NOB member. Moreover, during the year, three regional meetings with five other follow-up schools were organized. The emphasis in those meetings was on the exchange of experiences with colleagues from classes of the same age-groups in the other schools. The general opinion about these meetings can be characterized as "interesting but not so useful", because the situation in the other schools was perceived as too different.

The pattern of collaboration among teachers within the school was intensive, especially among teachers within grade levels. The more hesitant teachers were thereby often stimulated by more enthusiastic colleagues. The principal often served as an internal consultant. He made a good match with the NOB developer; there was mutual respect and affinity.

In the next school year (1987-88), the visits of the NOB member became less frequent. The principal increased his efforts to coordinate the activities, trying to prepare the entire teaching staff for more final decision making. He tried to anticipate teachers' potential problems and to solve them, thereby diminishing the risk that individual teachers would feel an inclination to "step out." Many resources were made available for the science lessons; the school has no shortage of money.

In the spring of 1988, an official decision was made by the entire staff of teachers to institutionalize the NOB approach, so that all of them were formally committed. The planning agreements were written down in the science part of the school work plan described earlier.

Institutionalization

Since the 1988-89 school year, the program has been in full action. The external NOB support has stopped completely. The principal is still serving as an internal facilitator and agent for change, striving towards "automation" of lesson preparation. He recognizes that the lengthy and complex lesson preparation is still a major problem for many teachers, and is perhaps an obstacle to continuation for some of them. As a possible solution, he proposes "lesson boxes" (or "kits") that should make it feasible to prepare a lesson in about 10 minutes (given a certain degree of experience). Each kit would contain all necessary resources for a lesson or a short series of related lessons:

- the print lesson-description;
- written background information about the subject matter;
- worksheets for the students;
- instruction charts for the teachers;
- all other specific objects or materials to be used.

As of the 1989-90 school year, the new program is still on the right track. Every third month the progress is evaluated at a staff meeting. Final decisions are taken about the specific kits to be made. The principal wants to be sure that the production of kits arises from stable choices after repeated experience. Each teacher has to deliver a list of priorities, on the basis of which the principal and assistant principal hope to make a number of basic kits. Time and money have been budgeted for this purpose.

The principal hopes that the availability of the kits will stimulate and help the teachers to continue their science activities, especially by diminishing the time and trouble of lesson preparation. He expects that the school needs another 3 years of continued experience with the activity-based approach before a secure state of institutionalization will be realized. By that time the teachers must be able to articulate their own approach and to specify their wishes for adaptation. If the teaching staff can then agree upon a new document concerning the school's approach to science, trust may be put in the future of activity-based teaching.

Explaining Institutionalization

Some of the factors behind the relatively successful process of implementation and (beginning) institutionalization of the activity-based approach in science teaching and learning at this school are as follows:

- The principal—combining expertise, enthusiasm, and organizational skills—served as a very effective and continuous internal agent for change.
- The external on-site support from the NOB developer was effective in stimulating and facilitating the initial implementation stage.
- The intensive collaboration patterns of teachers in various combinations provided much professional and social support for the teachers in their efforts to master the new tasks and roles, and to overcome obstacles in their path.
- The process of decision-making was careful, with serious efforts to solve real problems, avoidance of harsh compulsion or confrontation, and mild social pressure. The process culminated in an official agreement and the planning of activities in written form.
- The implementation process reflects the notion that the most fruitful strategy for achieving commitment by the entire teaching staff has two complementary components: assistance to the learning process of individual teachers, and stimulation of the social learning process of the group.
- When the above conditions were met, the activity-based approach had the opportunity to prove its inherent attractiveness and value, thereby becoming an intrinsic cause for change.

Chapter 5

A German Case: Birkenwaldschule

The search for schools with exemplary activity-based science education was assisted by the Institute for In-Service Teacher Training in Hamburg. The head of its department for elementary science teaching nominated three schools which met the IMPACT criteria and from which choices could be made. The Birkenwaldschule elementary school (pseudonym), located in a suburban area, was selected as one of the German cases. After discussing the aims of the study and its practical importance with the principal, permission to conduct the case study was obtained.

Data Collection

Data collection in Birkenwaldschule extended over 2 weeks and included observation of classes, interviews with five teachers, and repeated interviews with both the principal and assistant principal. An interview was also conducted with the coordinator of the *Lernwerkstatt*, a resource and learning center in the school, which is a place for in-service education and has a separate small printing office. An extended photographic documentation of learning activities was prepared to illustrate the many teaching and learning practices.

School Characteristics

As a result of its long-time reputation regarding open education, Birkenwaldschule is well known in the area and regularly visited by teachers, in-service trainers, trainees, and principals of other schools in the Hamburg area—and even from other states. Even though it has a reputation for exemplary practice, it does not have extra funds at its disposal for specific innovative efforts. At the time the case study was conducted, the school had a total of 305 pupils in 15 classes, with three or four classes per grade and an average of 20 pupils per class. The staff consisted of 19 teachers, some with part-time contracts.

Innovation profile

The core aim of this school is to strengthen the child's ability to direct his or her own activities and to learn how to learn. Learning through practical work and discovery of natural phenomena are central to this approach, which is now practiced in more than 50 primary schools in the Hamburg area. Special attention is paid to the changing social conditions of the children's lives, some of which are limiting. Psychological stress, TV watching, and the number of one-parent families is increasing, whereas direct exploration of natural settings and other opportunities for personal development have deteriorated; positive social contact and emotional development are under growing risk (cf. Schwarz, 1989, p. 5ff). As in two IMPACT cases, the activity-based approach to open education was introduced in the form of daily and weekly plans, (*Tages- und Wochenplans*). A weekly plan identifies learning activities for all, some parts of which are choices at the disposal of each student. Depending on which teacher is teaching, it comprises 25% to 50% of the total teaching time.

Activity-based learning is a traditional element of area schools which, in some cases, goes back to the 1920s. The syllabus recommends a great deal of activity-based studies in all subjects. Emphasis is placed on natural inquiry methods, technical issues and on constructing products with various materials.

Educational rationale

The principal and vice-principal both emphasize the constant need for pedagogical encouragement, which stimulates rather than controls *all* children, not just the highly motivated ones. This pedagogical encouragement requires an open, productive school climate. Tolerance, openness, and mutual support are part of this climate. The principal and the staff foster a school climate in which everybody can feel comfortable and be honestly accepted; it places great emphasis on continued efforts to make improvements: "Our school is a place where adults, not just students, are continuously learning," says the assistant principal.

Innovations are introduced in moderate steps so that everybody has sufficient opportunity to assimilate what is new; "quick shots" are rejected. In Birkenwaldschule, experiences with activity-based learning are frequently discussed among the staff, as well as being presented to and clarified for the parents and the public. As the principle explains, "We have improved our school step by step. Experiences with activity-based learning styles were mutually exchanged and discussed in detail with parents before taking the next steps." And the speed of innovation is carefully matched with the capacity of students to grow with the new, to master it and recognize gains.

Organizational context

The attendance area of the school is limited to the district of the city in which it is located. Children from other areas can also attend the school if special requirements are met. About 20% come from one-parent families and another 10% have non-German parents. The school itself consists of standard buildings, with large grassy areas, an adventure playground, and biotopes.

The classrooms contain various activity areas. Learning materials are in boxes and cabinets and on tables; in corners and on shelves, read-

FIGURE 5-1
Adventure Playground

ily accessible to every child. There are tables for group work; a discussion area for all; library shelves and resource corners; a sitting and theater area; and tables along some of the walls for displaying the students' work. The classrooms are relatively spacious, because the number of pupils has dropped from an average of 30 to an average of 20 per class during preceding years, as has happened in all elementary schools in the Hamburg area. The learning environment is very attractive, comfortable, and can be rearranged as needed. A learning studio is part of the stimulating learning environment of the school and is located in a classroom in which an impressive printing system has been installed. Evidently, it has become a tradition to produce many products using printing techniques, and thus make the students more versatile in producing printed products (e.g., Project Week reports, newsletters, and other items.)

Work with parents

Parents are substantially involved in school life. They assist during lessons, supervise printing activities, assist the students in learning to

FIGURE 5-2
Prints Students Have Developed by Using Freinet Techniques

read, contribute to social activities in the school, provide information resources, and serve as consultants or helpers during the annual Project Week. Most parents agree with the innovative rationale of the school, though there are still a few who seem to be disconcerted. These parents complain that children might "go off the rails," and that they as parents will be unable to control them any longer; or they complain that their children no longer have any homework. Some of those who think this way remain skeptical; most support the work done at school, however. The principal concedes that there is a persistent need for parent-oriented clarification, but the vast majority of parents are supportive.

Teaching staff

The teachers are skilled with activity-based learning. The roots of activity-based learning in this particular school go back more than seven years, to when the pioneers first explored how activity-based learning could be introduced into the life of the school. No teacher in Birkenwaldschule has received pre-service education in the science domain of general studies. Despite this lack of background, everyone teaches general studies, including science, issues of technology, and craft work. Ongoing in-service education covers a wide range, and includes: educational week-end conferences; annual meetings; visiting schools in other cities; participating in national and international workshops about Freinet pedagogy; and participating in Gestalt pedagogy courses and supervision.

The school curriculum

Compulsory schools in the Federal Republic of Germany are bound to syllabi or guidelines set up by each state, and this is the case in Hamburg. Central to activity-based learning in science is the general studies syllabus for Hamburg elementary schools (1980) and the elementary school syllabi for social studies and general studies (1980, 1986). Inquiry learning is given a clear priority in these documents. Learning is expected to be linked with the environment of the school and with the children. Experiences such as the trip to school, leisure time, the bakery, the recreation area in the neighborhood, nature settings, and downtown or the museum represent learning opportunities in which the active involvement of the student is fostered.

Learning by doing is well established. Activities include such projects as: preparing a photo exhibition about playgrounds; designing a chart; inventing tools; developing a noise map for a familiar area; or painting a series of pictures about the harvest or banana transport. The elementary school curriculum is based on these principles—yet differentiated and supplemented by the ideas of each individual school.

Learning materials

Educational games, textbooks, and craft books, flash cards, all kinds of files, worksheets, building sets and technical models, experimental aids, plasticine, printing systems, newspapers and documentation resources are regularly used media. Within the syllabus for general studies (1986) constructive work is considered to be of high value because the products of pupils shows what they have understood and in what manner.

ACTIVITY-BASED LEARNING IN PRACTICE

Teaching patterns in the school vary according to the teachers' individual preferences. Nearly all teachers favor activity-based teaching methods within the context of weekly plans and offer alternative learning activities to the students who make their own choices. Although there are instructional differences among the classes, the following similarities have been identified: (a) pupils' motivation to become involved in self-directed learning is high and constant; (b) activity-based learning is not limited to weekly-plan teaching—it is also found in other lessons; (c) group work and mutual assistance among the students are conducted with competence.

As in the other IMPACT case studies, the extent to which various elements of activity-based learning have been implemented is of direct interest. Based on classroom observations, document analysis, and interviews, the following elements are addressed, and descriptions provided of the extent to which they are present.

Planning

The students formulate meaningful questions of their own to investigate an area of nature or technology. The activity-based pattern of instruction involves the student in goal setting, project planning, reflecting upon experiences, contributing ideas for studying nature or other phenomena, and designing and constructing a product.

Evidently, self-directed discovery cannot be implemented without planning. Children first discuss what they want to do, then collect ideas and use their own experiences. The *Morgenkreis*, the weekly plan, and free-choice activities, provide opportunities to do this. The weekly plan is given to the children on Mondays. It is usually divided into three parts: (a) compulsory, (b) optional, (c) spare time. On the basis of this, the pupils plan what they want to do and when. Motives for setting priorities vary. One of the pupils, Frank, said, "If you always get homework and do not have a weekly plan, the teachers decide what you do when; we have got to decide that for ourselves now." Another student, Elsa, indicated that "you have to learn how to do it, but once you have learned how to use the weekly plan it is quite easy." Somebody else added, "After 3 weeks we could do it." Yvonne said, "I think the weekly plan is especially good because you can decide when to do things yourself. Once I went to school in France, and there you always have to do certain things at certain times. Here, one person does spelling while others are doing math, and you can decide for yourself. And if you do not manage to do something in school you have to do it at home."

Exploring

The students specify their ideas as to how their questions can be investigated, how light can be shed on them, and on how they can be reformulated and answered. At this level, discovery processes among 9- to 10-year-olds encompass activities such as observing, caring for plants, comparing, or constructing ecological aids for animal protection. The students conduct research activities, some of which stem from their own suggestions about inquiry procedures.

The pupils are able to use the discovery method well. They know what is important when doing simple experiments, how to observe and take notes, and that precision is also important. What they investigate, explore by construction, or observe, is specified in the exemplary lessons which follow this section.

Understanding

Exploration requires the repeated attempt of the learner to understand what she or he is seeing and learning. For this purpose, the students formulate their observations, express them, indicate interesting phenomena, analyze and examine their own interpretations based on their previous conceptions, discuss important findings within the context of experiments or in connection with various kinds of products they have made themselves. Sometimes they may be assisted by the teacher or other students, but help is given as a learning aid, not as a ready-made solution.

On the experimental level, biological themes are central if not predominate. (In other schools the same phenomenon can be observed; cf. the Dutch case.) The pupils know how to formulate and record obser-

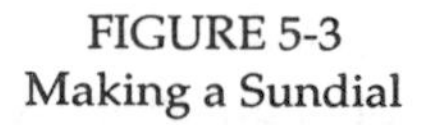

FIGURE 5-3
Making a Sundial

vations. They try to understand what they see by deliberative discussion and tentative hypotheses. Sometimes they ask the teacher in order to ascertain which of their guesses are correct. Of highest importance to the interviewees is learning to learn—understanding by doing things and finding out. Learning is usually interdisciplinary, which enables pupils to realize that subjects are multi-faceted. Basic abilities taught in this way are acquired in a non-analytical context.

Evaluating

The students analyze and systematize. They express and interpret what they have explored, constructed, or encountered. They draw conclusions, compare results with what they had expected, and submit proposals for further activities. They communicate and display their results during school or on other occasions.

One of the lessons we observed culminated in finding sorrels—not in a book, but in nature. Another involved, not specialist information about a bakery, but students making their own bread and eating it together. Producing and constructing stimulates the children to tell others about what made them excited, and about the problems they solved; children's reports about their results are always lively and interesting. They can literally *show* what they have achieved and produced. This is the most direct source of motivation. Nearly every activity or project ends with something concrete and involves planning it, analyzing it, and telling others about it. Results are recorded in writing, for example: in worksheets; in posters and stories about investigations; and in booklets about nature and about things made in craft lessons, such as hot air balloons or cookies.

Activity overview

Inquiry methods are common in the observed classes; activities within the following domains are written on a special board in each classroom:

- astronomy,
- aeronautics,
- rocks,
- motors,
- hot air balloons,
- flying objects,
- restoration of a river.

Such projects are routine at this school. During a visit to the Project Week exhibit, projects were viewed in which technical and scientific themes were integrated into interdisciplinary topics, such as:

• *Sound studio.* Pupils from the third and fourth grades had visited a TV and sound studio as a preparatory part of producing their own radio play, which they wanted to record on tape the next day. They learned something about labial sounds, and about synchronization and the individual stages which it involves; a "take" was explained, and the ways in which the editor and the actors can react to one another immediately was shown on a monitor. The training of a sound technician was explained. Finally the children asked the editor, the presenter, and a dubbing actor how they could produce sounds themselves for their own radio play, and were given useful tips.

• *Rotating disco lanterns.* Other students made rotating disco lanterns at school from balloons wrapped with fine rope and squares of shiny paper. At the same time, others from the same group worked on lighting technology.

- *Stalls.* Two girls painted stalls which their group had made from wooden laths and sheets of wood with an awning to cover it.
- *Machines for catching balls.* In another classroom, a machine for catching balls had almost been finished. It was approximately 1.2 meters high, pyramidal, and colorfully painted, with a hole at the front big enough for a tennis ball. A tube from this hole led back out again at the bottom front.
- *Soundproof barrier.* The principal reported that in 1986, the initiative which led to the construction of a soundproof barrier between the schoolyard and the adjacent motorway came out of Project Week. (Parents provided the signatures which the children collected.)
- *Spiders.* In the previous Project Week, the children had dealt with various scientific and technical themes. For example, one pupil reported the following about spiders: "We caught spiders for a short while, observed them and looked up what they eat. Somebody once told me that garden spiders are supposed to be dangerous and that they only live in Africa, but it is exactly the opposite: they live here and they are not dangerous."
- *Building sailing ships. Endangered species.* One student reported that "On the day of the project I put water into a large wooden dish. We had to build a sailing ship out of polystyrene and make an incision into it at the back. We then had to place liquid soap onto the water and the ship moved. Then we did some more research about pandas and about endangered species."
- *Environmental protection.* Another student reported that "Once we also did some research on environmental protection and I thought it was very good. We had a table and we could put things in it about trees, about water, and various other things. I once did some research about water. We tried various things, liquid soap and salt, to see how they could be cleaned and so on. I thought that was good; it was interesting."

Children plan and make their own things from materials of their own choice. They use encyclopedias, compendia, worksheets, weekly plans, newspaper articles, and occasionally, text books. They are introduced to chemistry by baking biscuits and bread rolls, collect old materials as part of a project about environmental protection, and make hypotheses about what is inflammable and dangerous or what is unsuitable for recycling. Children especially enjoy finding out about natural things, as by examining a damaged bird's egg or observing ants. Sometimes they do research at home, in the school library, or by interviewing people with a cassette recorder.

Exemplary lesson A. Class 4b consists of 24 pupils. The pupils gather on Monday for a morning circle. The discussion is non-directed; they communicate by giving signs to each other which are accepted by everyone, including the teacher. For example: both hands raised means, "I should like to comment on the topic"; one hand raised means, "I have a new topic to discuss"; one hand, thumb up means, "It is too loud, I can't understand."

The morning circle is an especially stimulating and popular method for the pupils—and the teacher—to inform the others of their experiences, wishes, and feelings, and for making suggestions. This discussion leads to important issues for further weekly-plan work and gives a picture of how the children feel. In one 45 minute period the following topics were mentioned, many of which are associated with nature and technology. The pupils talk, evaluate, listen to what the others have to say, and make their own contributions:

- found fish and dead starfish;
- got a soccer star's autograph;
- participated in a skateboard competition;
- found a cave in the sand dunes;
- saw a dead seal in Denmark;
- discussed European election;
- found fish on the Danish coast;
- detected cement bunkers on the coast;
- reported about one's own dance group;

The following periods and days were devoted to "Hamburg" as the weekly subject, including excursions downtown.

Exemplary lesson B. Class 4b consists of 20 pupils. The weekly plan has five activities that all pupils should cover:

1. write two 5-minute texts
2. prepare worksheets from the red history tray
3. complete your picture story
4. study "nature in the city"
5. prepare worksheets from the green tray

Four periods were observed in this class. Several collages about "Nature in the City" resulted from the group work. The children investigated the places in the city where they could find animals and plants. They used manuals and reference books. When asked, the teacher gave advice and hints on how to continue. This unit within the weekly plan is an example of how children use easily accessible sources of information.

The integrated teaching which is routine practice here has a number of significant results. Children develop understanding best by making things, writing, reading, and above all by advising one another, working together, and making observations. A bird's egg, which somebody had brought to school, was preserved, put onto the experiment table in the classroom and examined with a magnifying glass. Some other children found ants under a stone on the playground, put them into a can filled with sand, and covered it with a sock—which was permeable to air—so that later they could observe the ants without disturbing them. In addition, many plants were exhibited in vases and jars. In this way, the children could compare what they saw with what was said about these natural objects in reference books.

A final circle in the class is illustrative of the children's mode of work. The children gather in a circle, display their products in the middle of the classroom, and report group by group on their work and findings. This form of interactive evaluation gets enthusiastic participation because the students are proud of what they have achieved and are appreciated for it; they are satisfied because they have finished a series of experiences and other activities in a productive way. The week's products include: a hot air ballon, picture stories, baked rolls, and a climbing woodpecker on a wooden pole.

The items found in this typical classroom include the following:

1 educational aids	2 black board
3 pin board	4 sideboard
5 teacher's desk	6 cage
7 desk	8 material display
9 pin board/pictures	10 desk
11 flowers	12 printing set
13 recreation zone	14 self-made cookies
15 stove	16 refrigerator
18 cupboard	19 material shelves
20 cupboard	21 tools
22 experimental equipment	23 semi-open shelves
24 paintings	

Learning impact

The pupils in Birkenwaldschule quickly grew accustomed to weekly-plan teaching; interviews with third- and fourth-grade pupils show that they prefer the open-educational approach to more traditional forms. Classroom observation, test sheets, and project documents indicate both a high level of independent creative learning and mastery of

FIGURE 5-4
Typical Classroom in Birkenwaldschule

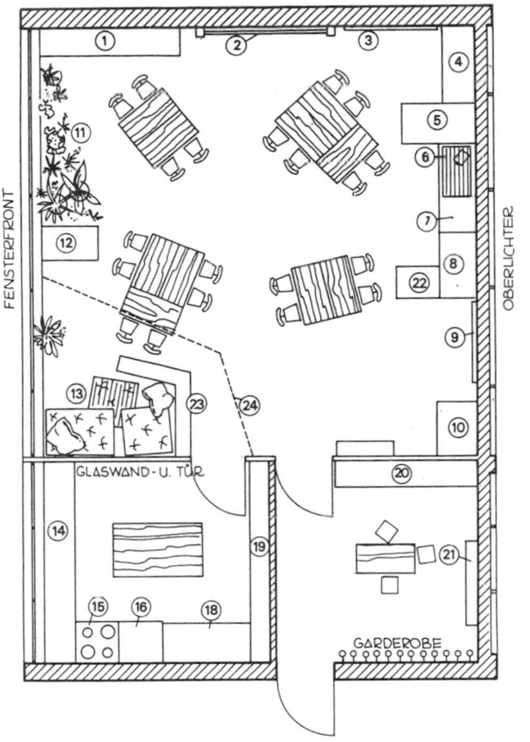

1 educational aids
2 black board
3 pin board
4 sideboard
5 teacher's desk
6 cage
7 desk
8 material display
9 pin board/pictures
10 desk
11 flowers
12 printing set
13 recreation zone
14 self-made cookies
15 stove
16 refrigerator
18 cupboard
19 material shelves
20 cupboard
21 tools
22 exper. equipment
23 semi-open shelves
24 paintings

more classical tasks. Most pupils develop sound competencies in organizing their own work, evaluating experiments, or constructing such items as a sun dial or launching a small hot air ballon.

The pupils gain increasing autonomy in sharing common tasks and responsibilities, communicating what they have found, inventing technical constructions, or implementing personal proposals for exploring nature. Conversations with children during our study showed them to be creative thinkers, producers of stimulating new ideas, and inventive explorers of nature and other phenomena.

We did not collect classical test data because primary schools in Germany typically do not use such tests. Instead, we analyzed the students' workbooks, the products of various student projects, documents about parental opinion and support, and various data from focused interviews. This evaluation showed that such learning outcomes are not only highly valued, but relatively stable.

Among their activities, pupils measure weather phenomena; investigate the life under stones; study ants; and determine the kinds of animals living in urban areas. Some groups explore the market, while others deal with their pets and how to care for them; everybody participates in printing a book about a topic of his or her concern. Topics such as dinosaurs; designing musical instruments; baking and cooking; weaving and macrame; repairing bicycles; pottery; and computers are familiar to the students of this school.

The headmaster reports that in addition to developing a lasting motivation to explore life and nature—learning by reflective doing is the educationale rationale here—the students become proficient in working together to systematically finalize projects. Students with learning difficulties have the opportunity to make significant progress in learning. Parents are impressed and convinced by the pedagogical richness of the student work.

A primary-school study by Schwarz, who was formerly responsible for primary schools in the Ministry of Education in Hamburg, produced similar results about this type of instruction: the children like going to school, they have learned to conduct their own studies, their passive behavior decreases, their ability to cooperate grows, they know how to interact harmoniously with others, and their capacity to concentrate has grown noticeably (Schwarz, 1989, p. 12). Activity-based learning through discovery in an open-education context is an integrated concept, which, when implemented, prepares children for learning.

The job satisfaction of teachers clearly increased under the new forms of teaching and has remained at this new level. The teachers at Birkenwaldschule feel at ease; they do not experience serious stress from the children or from the classroom situation. They see the fruit of their work in the children—in their excitement and motivation, their creativity and willingness to cooperate, their learning how to learn, and in their involvement in the class. The teachers have learned to help one another, to accept criticism from colleagues, and above all, to get the best out of the children. The educational value of lessons at this school is found in the productive tension between understanding and challenging; supporting and encouraging; intervening moderately and knowing when to leave students to their own devices. The role of a teacher at Birkenwaldschule is now quite different from that of years ago. Planning, advising, helping, moderating, and checking are required every day, and are far more important than other administrative tasks.

In the school as a whole, satisfaction with activity-based methods has grown. The climate of the school is relaxed, stimulating and cooperative. Aggression among pupils has decreased. The positive effects of activity-based learning and open education are visible not only in the students' achievement but also in their commitment to active work which, in turn, creates a very positive image of the school—particularly because disadvantaged students achieve considerable success.

History of Activity-Based Learning

The following paragraphs contain a sketch of the process by which activity-based learning emerged in Birkenwaldschule, and how it was finally incorporated into school life and daily routine.

Debut/initiation

Why did the school start or intensify activity-based learning in science, and how did it happen?

Over 10 years ago, two teachers began using open forms of teaching. At that time the following factors were decisive, and to a certain extent still are: (a) the children's changing environment, (b) the influence of learning about Freinet's work, and (c) growing dissatisfaction with conventional teaching. A short time later another teacher followed, all of them supported by the school principal.

The school board has always supported their work and continues to do so. The activity-based learning approach in the context of open education seemed to be long overdue. The syllabus provided a welcome opportunity to approach discovery learning through self-guided work in science and technology. Inspectors were invited, together with headteachers from other schools and the senator for education in Hamburg.

Two teachers indicated in interviews a fascination with Freinet's pedagogical thought since their student days. Their distinct openness to new ideas facilitated initiatives on the classroom level. The assistant principal began 4 years ago, partly because she was impressed by what had been achieved so far, partly because of her educational affinity for open methods of teaching, and partly because of the apparent practicality of the innovation. The visibility of the innovation within the school and its stimulating impact on the students soon caused others to try the new approaches. Having two staff members per class facilitated mutual exchange and assistance, a situation that existed in 3 out of 20 classes at that time.

A careful inventory of how the classes functioned and of the child's home situation preceeded every step towards change; it created the basis for further steps. This basis expressed itself not only in the weekly-plan model but also in the greatly changing role of the teacher and in the development of new patterns of interaction among pupils and teachers. Special emphasis was placed on how the children lived, since many children lived in very small apartments and came from unstable families. The "old" form of learning was difficult for children with such problems; the time was ripe for a new kind of education.

Exploratory tryout

How did the teachers, principal, students, parents, administrative authorities and external support professionals become acquainted with the new approaches? What did they do, adopt, or decide to facilitate during tryouts? What premises had to be taken into account? What was achieved up to that point?

The lessons were restructured and opened up in many ways; there was a new role for the teacher and there were no grades in the report cards.

However, the open teaching as implemented did not always meet participants' expectations, according to the assistant principal. During the exploratory phase, alternative ways of organizing open teaching and activity-based learning in science and technology were tried out. Among the innovations tested were the following: weekly plans, morning circles, closing circles, free-choice activities, project work, various research activities, excursions, and class councils.

Currently, project work and other explorative learning based on an interdisciplinary selection of topics from nature and technology occurs about once a week. The pupils choose their means of discovering, investigating, "doing something," producing, or building which are a major part of every project. The children work daily with various materials available in the classroom or brought in on agreement.

Several project activities and models emerged from the exploratory period, which are often used by teachers in this school and other schools. The pupils report that they enjoy producing their own project notebooks and reports; their enjoyment in producing their own work is often more intense than in using prefabricated equipment.

The collegial conversations in the school show that teachers are able to criticize each other without hurt feelings. This reflective sensitivity contributes to a lasting cooperative school climate. Even more important is the readiness of the staff to change behavior according to new knowledge. The principal tries to encourage his staff both to continue exploring and to stabilize successful practice. He promotes the new ideas in conferences again and again. He is concerned with strengthening a feeling in everyone of being personally responsible for the happiness of the students.

Implementation

Who contributed to the implementation of activity-based learning, and in what way? What did the process of implementation look like? What sort of external support was provided when the new approach was conceived as a process of reconstructing current practice?

The principal and assistant principal both said that, especially in the beginning, reservations about open teaching were due to a lack of knowledge about the new method. This is why the school quickly intensified its public relations. School supervisors, principal, parents, associations, and members of the Hamburg community—those in favor of the innovation and those against it—were invited to visit the school to get an authentic picture of the changes. The school hoped to bring the debate back to an unemotional level; as a result, understanding grew. Some critics were thus better able to comprehend the innovation.

Political opposition developed during the restructuring and a number of problems needed solving. As a result, the school has given close attention to public relations since that time. It soon became clear, however, that the school's capacity to handle this expanded communication process was limited. In particular, it was hard to handle the number of visitors from teacher-training seminars, colleges, and other schools who wanted to see open teaching in practice. Lasting forms of cooperation with colleges and teacher training institutions, however, did develop during restructuring.

Beginning routine

What indicated the emergence of an institutionalized pattern of innovation? What conditions encouraged repeated use? What difficulties had to be solved, and how? Who supported and stabilized the new routine?

The school has gained a good reputation. The fact that the second all-German learning studio meeting was held in Hamburg in 1989, and the fact that a growing number of people visit Birkenwaldschule, speak for themselves. The primary school is an ideal example of open teaching in Hamburg and beyond the city limits. The school's 10 years of experience is a plus. The most important organizational and contextual prerequisites of open schooling have become routine at the school. The new teaching approaches have become routine, and many teachers who want to update their teaching practices try to get positions at this school because they expect to learn to use new ideas.

Part of this new routine is improving practice through criticism and self-appraisal. One of the interviewees asked herself repeatedly whether everything was sufficiently organized or whether she should do more work toward organization. In a conversation with a doctoral student who did a thesis on this school, she mentioned that the weekly plan is a good framework but is not the source of educational innovation; success is far more dependent on changed patterns of interaction between teacher and pupil. Introducing open lessons and the weekly plan means "treating children differently according to a different view of learning" (Wallrabenstein, 1989, p. 20). The principal also referred to the teachers' self-concept. He said many were reluctant to "look into themselves" in the beginning but now engage in self-reflection in a professional way. This process requires a large amount of time and a high level of commitment.

Institutionalization

What was the sequence of events leading to institutionalization? What are the indicators of a routinized continuation of activity-based teaching? What happens after institutionalization?

The learning studio set up 2 years ago mirrors the variety of materials and the unique learning environment that can now be found in nearly every classroom of the school. A learning-studio teacher said that the teachers had become so skilled in developing materials that the learning studio is now in a position to open its services to external staff.

Another indicator of the success of self-sufficient, experimental learning at Birkenwaldschule is the increasing number of parents from other attendance areas who enroll their children in Birkenwaldschule, where the staff has agreed on the following educational guidelines.

- Every pupil is accepted and supported in his or her personal development.
- Educational interaction is guided by mutual respect and partnership.
- Continued learning is demanded of all teachers and is supported by various measures.

• In the context of consultative talks, student council, roundtable discussions, report cards, and other methods, pupils are given specific choices which lead them to accept responsibility for themselves.

• Individual learning progress should be the major basis for every child's success.

• The teachers should be knowledgeable learners and co-learners with the children.

The school has also developed, by a consensus of all staff members, a catalogue of essentials which, among other things, includes the following:

1. The child's curiosity should be awakened, maintained and promoted.
2. The child should be given room to develop growing responsibility for what he or she learns.
3. Learning should encompass the head, heart, and hands equally. Learning together and encouraging each other are central for both the students and the teachers.
4. Social learning is given the same importance as other learning: all members of the school accept one another, develop the ability to alter behavior and to pay attention to the appraisal of individual learning progress.

Another school document outlines the fundamental methods that are to be accepted by new colleagues. The school does not want to regress to previous practices. In short, the basics are:

1. A child can only learn efficiently if he or she is allowed to find his or her own method of learning.
2. The syllabus requirements are treated in the appropriate form and sequence if the above essential is given sound attention.
3. Activity-based learning requires a multitude of materials for the children. Techniques that enable children to investigate, to work creatively and productively, to practice what they have learned, and to control their own work individually and in groups are central to educational practice at Birkenwaldschule.
4. Exploring the reality outside the school is central and comprehensive (e.g., through projects and Project Weeks, working in the school garden or in biotopes, investigative activities, or inviting parents and experts into the class).
5. Choices and free work are necessary for the child's development, whether in the form of free activities in physical education, planned and self-determined division of work, or open recess.

Explaining Institutionalization

Some aspects of institutionalization will be addressed here, although the reader's attention is also directed to the cross-case analysis in chapter 9, where all cases are used as a comprehensive resource for findings and recommendations. The work of Birdenwaldschule is well documented and shows that activity-based learning has been substantially institutionalized over the past decade. Although the school does not have the special status often given to pilot projects or reform endeavors, the careful improvement process has made the school what it is today.

The excellent school climate and success of Birkenwaldschule has had an impact beyond the school itself. Other primary schools in the Hamburg area use similar methods today. To a certain extent, schools nearby were forced to do something, as so many children from their own attendance area were starting school at Birkenwaldschule. This development led these schools to consider how they could become educationally more attractive so they could compete with Birkenwaldschule.

When asked how they would advise a school or colleague wanting to embark on more activity-based learning, the principal and assistant principal offered the following suggestions: (a) Whoever wants to begin open teaching should strictly avoid trying everything at once. One or two areas of innovation are enough in the beginning, such as starting with general studies or activity-based learning in one's native language; (b) The new has to be reconciled with prevailing patterns of action, and probably also divided into digestible parts (compartmentalized), and reconceptualized according to local needs so that all the children will gain from it; (c) Project Weeks are appropriate starting points for exploring the extent to which the school is ready for activity-based improvements on an instructional level.

The initiative gained from the early activity of a few teachers in applying Freinet pedagogy was influential. These teachers opened doors to new ideas. The assistant principal made the new ideas available to the staff, and so visibility of the new approaches was guaranteed. Immediate implementation was supported and the proximity of innovation within the school helped to increase its credibility. The aims of the innovation were clarified for all, in time, and success was ensured as a stimulating environment was created. The children's own views were consequently more often elicited, and education was more powerfully anchored in the individual child. The self-confidence of the children was reinforced, which, in turn, helped them to master the challenges of self-guided learning found in activity-based patterns of instruction. Instructional variation inspired not only the children but also the parents and teachers; professional self-reflection was promoted. The new approaches were made accessible to all, as risk-taking and responsive thought and action were encouraged. Progress was steady as people were encouraged but not put under the pressure of time.

Lessons and practices which were meaningful to the children and related to experience were only available to a limited degree at first. However, once individual initiative was supported, discussion steadily increased and learning processes were initiated; the endeavor grew. It was necessary to formulate aims—for everyone's sake—not through a single act, but repeatedly and in a clear and solid fashion.

This process partly took the form of mutual guidance, in-service training, and the development of teaching materials. It rapidly caused other teachers to follow suit. Innovations were taking place at the school and everybody had the opportunity to get an insight into restructured lessons. The process fostered the conviction among more teachers that the new approach could be useful for their own lessons.

Knowledge about open lessons in isolation is not sufficient. One must be prepared to examine innovations, to become familiar with them, and in doing so to discover how they work. The resulting pragmatic knowledge becomes meaningful in the light of mutual investigation and critical appraisal.

Chapter 6

A Swedish Case: Linden School

Linden School (a pseudonym) was selected as one of the Swedish cases partially on the basis of previous knowledge about the school, having become aware of it in 1982 when it participated in a Nordic network of well-developed schools. Having not met people from the school during the past 2½ years, I checked with the school leader to see if the school was still working in the same direction that it had earlier. When he indicated it was, I checked with people belonging to the county board of education about their impression of the school; they said the school was using activity-based learning principles. A final check over the phone with the two leading teachers at the school about their actual working profile confirmed that it was still going strong.

Data Collection

Data gathered on this school included: observations of the work of children and teachers in the school context; interviews with teachers about the actual working pattern and the history of the working-pattern changes in Linden School; a telephone interview with the school leader who was in charge when the new working pattern was initiated; analysis of reports that the school had written on its own history in 1983, 1984, and 1986; and review of a large number of "week-books" written by the students of Linden School, to obtain examples of activity-based learning in science.

School Characteristics

Linden School is one out of four schools in the western school-management area of its *kommun*. This *kommun* has about 18,000 inhabitants and is located in the center of "Middle Sweden."

Linden School is situated in the small municipality of Linden, about 10 kilometers west of the center of the *kommun*, along the western railway going to Stockholm and Goeteborg, the major cities on the east and west coasts of the country. The dominating image of the *kommun* is that of the largest railway junction in Sweden. It is the point where a large north-south railway crosses the east-west railway. A large marshalling yard dominates the center of the *kommun*. The major industry is a factory that makes harvesting machines. There are also a brick industry, a cement plant, timber yards and smaller mechanical industries. In the municipality of Linden there are no industries; it is dominated by one-family houses.

Ten years ago the western school-management area contained eight school sites, but early in the 1980s these eight schools were consolidated. Today there are four school sites. The western school-management area is largely rural, and some of the smallest and most rural schools were closed; now the children that live in the outer parts of the *kommun* have to travel to their schools. In the western school-management area, there are schools only for students from the first through sixth grades of the *grund*-school. When the students begin a higher level, at Grade 7, they must go to one of the two schools elsewhere in the *kommun* which include that level. The office of the school leaders of the western school-management area is not located in Linden School but in a school some kilometers away.

The Linden School site was not involved in the consolidation that took place at the beginning of the eighties. The students that come to this school live in the municipality of Linden and its closest surroundings. The school has about 160 students in grades 1 through 6 and a preschool class is also located at the site, which means that 6-year-olds are also present there. About three out of four students come from homes of the small municipality of Linden and the others come from farms located at a distance of 2 to 5 kilometers outside of Linden. The students come from stable working class or middle class homes. In Linden there are very few immigrants.

There are three working units in Linden School. One is composed of three classes of the lower stage, in which the students are mixed so that a third of the 7-year-olds, a third of the 8-year-olds and a third of the 9-year-olds belong to the same class and are taught together most of the time during the school week. The three teachers with the main responsibility for these three classes cooperate in the flow of work. Grades 4 and 5 make up another working unit of the school, and the two sixth-grade classes constitute the last working unit. In this latter unit, students of different ages work cooperatively much less often during a typical week than do the younger students.

The school site is divided into two distinct parts. One is used as a learning area mainly by the lower stage of the school and the other one mainly by the middle stage. The local library and the Folkets Hus society are located in a third part of the school site. Folkets Hus societies were born in Sweden about a hundred years ago. They are parts of the workers' movement and occupied with arrangements of informal education, political meetings, and pure entertainment among local people. The meeting areas of the Folkets Hus society are used by the children when they eat their daily meal. All-school meetings of the students are also held there. Because the local library and the Folkets Hus society are in the same building, many activities take place in the school building after school hours, in which some of the children participate. Theater groups meet in the Folkets Hus' part of the building in the late afternoons and the children, as well as their parents, go to the library in the afternoon to find books to read during their spare time. The facilities of the Folkets Hus society are one of the natural meeting points in the community.

Thirteen teachers work at Linden School: seven class teachers, two special teachers, and four subject specialists, who teach the children handicrafts and physical education. These specialists spend only a couple hours per week at the school. The local working plan of Linden School states as a basic principle that teachers working with students are to help them feel secure, foster tolerance in their thinking, and keep their curiosity alive. On the basis of these ideas, the school days are organized such that students of the third and fourth grades spend one or more afternoons during the week doing some kind of research of their own, or doing research that their teachers initiate. Their research covers science topics as well as studies of society, human relations and many other subject areas.

Activity-Based Learning in Practice

The profile of activity-based learning in the school varies to some degree depending on which teacher is in charge of the third or fourth grade. The normal pattern of organizing a school in Sweden is that teachers concentrate on a class of students that they follow during a three year period. Usually these students are born during the same year, i.e. in 1987. After the first three years of schooling another teacher becomes responsible for the same class of children during the next three years, and during the last three years of the *grund*-school a group of subject teachers deals with the same class for the last three year period. A teacher of the lower stage therefore usually deals with third graders only each third year. In Linden the lower stage is organized for multi-grade teaching, which leads to all lower stage teachers working together with the third graders every year. The organization of the middle stage at Linden is more traditional, which means that the teachers of that stage are responsible for the fourth graders every third year.

The interviews and observations indicated a mixture of the major characteristics of student work described in chapter 2. Sometimes the students formulate their own research questions, sometimes they follow proposals put forward by the teachers, and other times they work with fairly direct teacher questions, which mainly come from learning materials. The students usually elaborate the results of their research and organize a display for others. It is a tradition at the school that results are presented to persons other than classmates—such as parents or people of the municipality—in the library area. The students often report their findings to students of classes other than their own, which comes rather naturally in this small school where the teachers have tried for a long time to break down the boundaries between age-groups. Learning aids such as books are sometimes used in the research work of the students, but the dominant pattern in this school is for the students to search for information in real life or in nature itself. The teachers favor producing learning materials with the students rather than depending on prefabricated materials.

Examples of science investigations in which the students are involved during their third and fourth years of schooling at Linden School include the following:

- how airplanes fly;
- what time is;
- how to make weather observations;
- how to measure temperature;
- the human body and its functions;
- energy, mainly electricity;
- pollution.

When the students were investigating different ways of measuring temperature, they constructed, on the basis of their own study in books, simple thermometers using alcohol. One of the third graders describes the experiment in his "week-book"—a kind of logbook in which each student writes continuously during the first 3 school years at Linden School—as follows: "On Wednesday we made an experiment. We made a thermometer. First we took a film can. Then we made a hole in it. Then we put down a straw in the hole. After that we poured T-alcohol into it. We tightened it with pop-glue. We saw how the T-alcohol changed in the straw."

Another third-grader describes in her week-book her experimentation with electricity: "We have had technics. We made experiments. We had a bulb to light. We linked threads, lamps and batteries together. It worked." In some of the classes each of the students marks out a specific "nature-square" in a forest or meadow portion of the immediate environment of the school. During the year the students make observations of natural changes within their square and report to others about it.

More about student work

The 9-year-old Swedish students plan their week in a planning book at the beginning of each week. They write down the individual tasks they will do as well as collective work they are planning. Each student also makes notes in her or his personal "research book," a logbook in which students record findings about their experiments (e.g., with air or water), and about what they have found while pursuing questions of their own choosing (e.g., how dogs behave or how cars work). This research work is done periodically during a typical week, often during hours earmarked for *omvärlds-orientering* (environment orientation) as well as during other periods such as Swedish or math.

A couple of days per year are designated as "research days." Specific themes are chosen and the students work together in groups. The first day is used for the research itself, with the children formulating basic questions to pursue and designing methods of investigation. Later, the students report their findings to other students in the school, and sometimes make presentations to the parents as well.

The topics covered on research days vary and are not limited to science. On the latest research day at Linden the following topics were included: hedgehogs, stamps, snakes, horses, dogs, computers, donkeys, geneological research, cars, boat traffic, plants, rabbits, space, and sharks.

Through these investigations, the children not only learn about the self-selected topics, but also develop independence and learn to work cooperatively in a helpful manner. Since students of different ages work together during research days, younger students become more secure in the school situation and older students develop more responsiblity toward others.

Impact of activity-based learning

The outcomes of the activity-based learning are evident in the knowledge and actions of the students. They know a lot about things that happen in nature and in their society; they also trust their own ways of examining the world around them. Teachers receiving the students in the seventh grade at the next level of school testify, according to the school's leader, that the students of Linden have higher self-esteem and more facility in working independently than students coming from other feeder schools.

At Linden, the 10-year-old students usually engage in activity-based learning within a specific thematic frame for a lengthy period of time, such as spending 3 months studying energy. During each school week, the 10-year-olds spend only two to four school lessons on "research work." The 9-year-olds at Linden spend more of the week on research, and they also cover more topics. Activity-based learning is more fully integrated into the total educational process during the first three years of schooling as compared with the fourth to the sixth year of schooling. Experiential learning appears in every subject, all the time during the lower stage at Linden.

The learning outcomes are shown in many ways. With the help of the copy machine, the students produce many "books" in their research work. Such books can be found in many places in the school. Reports are displayed on classroom walls and in common areas. Photo series have also been produced. The corridors are not empty: the staff has placed tables in them so they can be used by groups of students doing research. In some classrooms there are reading corners. The walls are covered with the results of student work on various topics.

History of Activity-Based Learning at Linden School

Initiation

The history of activity-based learning at Linden School during the third and fourth years of schooling goes back more than a decade. In 1975, one of the teachers of the lower stage, who was rather critical of the working patterns in Swedish schools in general, started to use an alternative way of helping students to learn to read and write. This alternative method—called Läsning på Talets Grund (LTG) teaches reading on the basis of the student's own spoken words. Thus, it is based on cognitions that the children already have. This method supports the children in taking early initiatives in their own education; they formulate important messages about their own experiences using their own words. The teacher may ask her students what they thought and felt when they found snow on the ground in the morning. After a short discussion she asks the students to write down important words that they would use to write to somebody about the new snow. Picking up important words of the student's own vocabulary, she will build the learning of reading and writing on high motivation. The students deal with important messages that they have constructed themselves and which they fully understand. As they learn to read through analyzing the construction of their own written messages, the students learn to write important statements that can tell others something of what they have experienced themselves.

The teacher who wanted to revise her working methods began following the guidelines of the LTG method (Leimar, 1974). At the time, the LTG method was being discussed widely among lower-stage teachers in Sweden. In-service courses and articles about the method appeared. This teacher was supported in her work by the school leader, at the time, of the western school-management area. She soon found the method to be very profitable for the children and she became more and more goal-directed in her work. She saw that the method was not limited to the teaching of reading, but had relevance to many other aspects of school life. The children began to think for themselves before and after they made things, whatever the subject happened to be. When the children became acquainted with this method, they were eager to tell others about their experiences, in school as well as out of school. They started to use writing as an important means of communicating with others.

Another lower-stage Linden teacher became interested in the LTG method after a year, as a result of repeated conversations with her colleague who had begun using it. She started to use the method when she faced a new group of first graders some years later.

Implementation

Other teachers at Linden listened to the two enthusiastic teachers during the latter years of the seventies, but they were not themselves interested in changing their long-established working methods. They continued to use the dominant pedagogical strategy—the strategy of knowledge distribution—which is based largely on teacher-planned events, with students seldom or never contributing to the plan. The textbook is the dominant educational tool with this strategy. Students work individually on the same tasks at the same time and group work rarely occurs. Work sessions are dominated by teachers' presentations, with prefabricated learning materials generally used in place of reality itself as the students' learning resources. Knowledge tests are a common part of this strategy.

In 1981, some of the old teachers left Linden and some new teachers entered the scene. The old, stable role-patterns of the small school were opened up and it became possible for the teachers to discuss working methods in an open way. The current school leader became deputy school director of the *kommun* and a new school leader took over. The new deputy school director continued her contact with the school, and participated in several discussions with the teachers and the new school leader about the development of the working pattern of the school.

The new school leader organized some of the five study days as evaluation and planning days for the school-management area, with each of the four schools in the school-management area being asked to produce a local working plan. The request for working plans from each school-management area was part of a reformation of the entire *grund*-school of Sweden, decided on by Parliament in 1979. Together with his teachers, the leader of the western school-management area decided in the fall of 1981 to produce four different local working plans, one for each school site in the school-management area.

The local working plan occupied teachers at Linden School during 1982. In the spring they used study days for discussion of the overall aims of the *grund*-school. During evening sessions in the fall they engaged in self-evaluation and held discussions about alternative ways of organizing and working in their school. They tried to identify shared views on human beings, society and the nature of knowledge. "What are the shared values of teachers in the school," and "What should be done with these shared values?" and "How can we practice them together with our students?" were questions addressed during 1982. In 1983, the in-service training continued, with teachers meeting two evenings each month with the school leader to discuss school-development issues. Books were read and radical ideas were presented, scrutinized and often rejected.

Some of the ideas from this period, however, entered the working patterns of the school. The structure of the lower stage was remade and multi-grade teaching was started. When the same idea of age-integrated classes was presented to the students and parents of the middle stage, however, there was a strong reaction against it. The students and their parents did not want to have this system for the middle stage. The main argument against the idea was that it was too far from the structure of the higher stage that the students would soon enter. A compromise between the different factions was constructed so that work in the middle stage would occasionally be done in temporary mixed-age groups.

The age-mixing ideas at Linden were important for the practice of activity-based learning. When students work together in multi-grade groups they need to find tasks neither totally dependent on *läroplan* guidelines nor linked to prejudice among teachers about when students are ready to engage in certain types of learning.

In 1982, Linden School was invited to participate in a Nordic network of schools that had succeeded in their efforts to develop their working culture. The school accepted the offer. One of the important aspects of participation was producing reports on the school's own development. The first report was produced in 1982, with three others following in 1983, 1984, and 1986. The teachers say that writing the reports on their own school's development made them highly aware of what they were doing, and that this awareness helped them to act in a more planned and goal-directed way.

In the Nordic network, Linden School was also obliged to host visits from the other schools of the network, and they had opportunities to make study-visits to schools in the other Nordic countries. From 1983 to 1986, some of the Linden teachers made study visits to other countries and were reinforced in their thinking about how the life of their school could be designed. In particular, the idea of mixed-age grouping was reinforced, along with ideas of how students could direct their own learning in an experiential way.

The school leader of the western school-management area—who was interested in testing ideas of decentralization that were being discussed in Sweden at the time—designed a model for resource use under which each of the four school sites became more responsible for its own time and money budgets. The teachers of Linden were now, in 1983 and 1984, more responsible than ever for managing their own affairs; the school leader changed the budget pattern so that each school site could manage its own time and money. Earlier systems of budgeting had been based on subjects, and distribution decisions were kept away from teachers and dictated to school leaders. Now the teachers became more aware of the resources they had with which to do their job, and they felt more freedom to design their own time schedule and the way they worked together.

Institutionalization

As suggested in the previous section, the new patterns which developed had their origins in several factors, including these:

- the initiative among some of the teachers to develop new working methods for student learning;
- the influence of the idea of mixing students of different age-groups;
- demands from the school leader that the staff take more responsibility for their own time and money budgets;
- participation in the Nordic network;
- development of the local working plan, with concentration on security, tolerance and curiosity as basic principles behind the design;
- regular in-service training.

From 1984 on, the activity-based learning pattern has been used by all the students in Linden School on a regular basis, both in science and in other subjects.

Today, the activity-based learning pattern is self-evident in this school: "Yes, the students are involved in their own research every afternoon in my class," one of the lower-stage teachers said in her first interview. "We work in this way in our school," she said casually. Today the teachers testify that they are fully aware that they have a somewhat different working pattern than other schools in the *kommun*. But they see their way of working with children as the normal way: "We are only following the guidelines of the *läroplan*. It is bad that others don't," stated one teacher. The activity-based learning pattern at Linden is so self-evident today that it is one of the arguments as to why the time schedule is designed as it is.

EXPLAINING INSTITUTIONALIZATION

The activity-based learning in Linden School was clearly initiated by the teacher who first became interested in a new method of learning to read. This method, the LTG method, is a practical adaptation of activity-learning principles to the teaching of reading and writing. Upon observing this method in use, it is easy to see that its principles—basing learning on the thoughts and beliefs of the students—can be practiced in many other fields of learning. The teacher who first used it at Linden

School drew this conclusion, and began using its main ideas in other subjects. This teacher, who still works at Linden, played an important role in the change process. She stimulated her colleagues in the lower stage to follow her lead. She developed a close working relationship with the school leader and kept up contact with her when she became deputy school director of the *kommun*. She also has a close friendship with the most influential middle stage teacher, which was important in developing activity-based learning at that stage.

It is also evident, however, that external stimuli were important during the initiation of activity-based learning. The first user encountered the LTG method in her in-service training, and she read about the method as well. Furthermore, in-service education events, participation in a development project, staff changes, and demands from both the local school leaders and from the distant management of the Swedish school system (through the *läroplan*) have been important in advancing activity-based learning within the school's ideological debate. Sorting out the influence of each of these factors on the historical flow of events, however, seems to be impossible. I have to stay with the conclusion that they all interacted and worked together, with the effects of their interaction being particularly important. A factor that seems to have had only a minor influence on events has been the cross-school sharing of experience. This process seems to have been important for starting age-group integration at Linden School, but does not seem to have been important in the initiation of the activity-based working pattern.

The way teachers at Linden School became acquainted with the new working pattern differs among individuals. Friendships among teachers were influential, but more important was a need for change felt by some of the teachers—a need for *omväxling*. They were bored with the old way of doing things, so why not try something else? The way in which cooperation and discussion took place at the school also seems to have been important in the initiation and implementation process. Teachers at the school are few in number and eager to cooperate with each other. The enthusiastic way in which they discussed their school and their work during the years of 1982, 1983, and 1984 probably determined the outcome of the implementation. During their twice-monthly evening meetings, they discovered each others' basic values, beliefs and ways of reasoning. This knowledge seems to have helped the people of Linden School to create a safe and stimulating work situation, and is an explanation of their openness to using activity-based learning.

The strong influence of the school leaders in the western school-management area and their development of a managerial structure in the area were also important for developments in the school. Demands on the teachers from the school leaders, both to develop a local working plan for Linden School and, simultaneously, to deal with the budgeting of time and money, were put forward at the same time that a large amount of in-service education was given. Cooperation occurred and discussion flourished about the aims and ideology of the school. More than the usual number of demands and ideas were put into practice.

When analyzing this case, institutionalization is obvious: Physical space is reserved for activity-based learning. Classes know what times during the week they will spend on research work. Agreement on the continued existence of the working pattern is solid. In comparing Linden with a similar neighborhood school, the superintendent of the *kommun* found that the people of Linden had a rationale for what they wanted to do and could easily make themselves understood when seeking money for "extras" such as student travel expenses. When the people of Linden meet other school personnel, such as colleagues from other schools during study days, they show them that they really own their organizational design as well as the working pattern of the school. Other indicators of institutionalization, such as "built-in-ness," invisibility, and legitimacy of the activity-based learning, are also present.

The perception of the Linden School teachers that activity-based learning is "the way we do it," and the emphasis on it in the school's local profile, are indications of institutionalization. Furthermore, the working method is visible outside the school: Some lower-grade teachers occasionally make presentations in in-service education events to tell others about the way they are working in Linden School. To these teachers, the most important part of what they "sell" to others is the idea of mixed-age groups. The activity-based learning pattern is just a part of the picture presented when they appear in other schools as in-service presenters.

The biggest question about the institutionalization of activity-based learning at Linden School is whether or not it will survive and thrive with changes of personnel over a period of years. The two pioneers have been there for many years and will probably continue to teach there for the rest of their professional lives. A full test of the institutionalization of activity-based learning in this school may not be possible until they have left the school.

Chapter 7

*A U.S. Case: The Sheridan County School District**

As part of the IMPACT project, a variety of case studies of schools and school districts were conducted within the United States. The case study of the Sheridan County School District (pseudonym) reported here was selected for inclusion because its science program has been well-established for many years, is well institutionalized, and illustrates processes for achieving institutionalization. Furthermore, the large size of the district provides an interesting contrast to the case studies that individual schools presented in earlier chapters.

The Sheridan County School District is large in both land area and population. It covers roughly 800 square miles (or 2000 square kilometers) and has approximately 75,000 pupils enrolled in nearly 120 elementary- and secondary-level schools. Although largely suburban, the school district includes a limited amount of rural area as well.

The district has chosen to take a very centralized approach to the development and implementation of curricula, in sharp contrast to some other school districts, in which curricular matters are left largely to individual schools. District instructional specialists custom-design district-approved curriculum guides for all subjects and grade levels.

The qualifications that teachers in the Sheridan County schools bring with them at their initial employment is typical of American elementary school teachers. Their specific background in science is minimal—essentially that required as part of their general education in

* Appreciation is expressed to Beth Hower, who was the co-investigator on this case study.

obtaining a bachelor's degree. A survey of teachers in the two schools indicated that the typical teacher had taken a course on the teaching of science in his or her teacher-preparation program and had taken an average of 2.7 content courses in the natural sciences.

DATA COLLECTION

Sheridan County contains Perris and Western elementary schools (pseudonyms) which were studied intensively as part of this case study. In addition to studying these two elementary schools, the researchers investigated a variety of district activities as well. They attended district in-service education classes, interviewed a variety of district personnel (including three members of the district science staff, the director of the district's in-service education program, two principals from other schools, an administrator in charge of approximately twenty of the district's schools, and two teachers from other schools who had played a role in district science improvement endeavors), and reviewed many documents, including curriculum guides.

SCHOOL CHARACTERISTICS

The science curriculum

For the reader familiar with U.S. elementary school science curriculum materials, the Sheridan County schools science program can be succinctly described as a collection of units from the *Elementary Science Study* (ESS) and *Science Curriculum Improvement Study* (SCIS) programs, modified to make a district program. These units have been woven into a total program extending from Grades 3 through 6, and provided with substantial support materials. All of the manipulative materials required for the program are carefully identified, and an extensive teachers' guide—which goes beyond the original units in terms of information for the teacher and suggestions for conducting classes—has been prepared for each grade level. Each of the units has been adapted to fit the district's program and, in addition, a few units of the district's own have been developed.

The program is clearly intended to be one which is activity-based as defined by the IMPACT project. The actual program as found in school practice is described in the following section.

Perris elementary

Perris Elementary School is located in a suburban area where the students come mostly from middle and upper-middle class homes. As is typical of public schools in the United States, virtually all of its students are in this particular school because they live within the geographic area which the district has defined as the school's attendance area. The teachers are primarily middle- aged (35-50)—seasoned professionals who have been with the school district for 10 to 25 years. The majority of them have spent many of those years at Perris, so there is a high degree of familiarity among the staff. The social climate of the school is warm, positive, and calm.

The students at Perris are outgoing and well-behaved. They respond well to the teacher-directed style that prevails in most classrooms. The classrooms become more active and the students more animated during their science period. The degree of freedom and movement varies from room to room depending upon the teacher's level of comfort with noise and with the students' independent decision-making. The smallest class size for science is about 20 students; the largest class size is in the low thirties.

While most of the teachers view science as one of their least favorite subjects to teach, they all recognize that it is one of the students' favorite content areas. Teachers believe that the opportunity for self-discovery, the direct manipulation of materials, and the chance for peer interaction are the main reasons for the positive status of science among students. Even though most of the teachers admit to a lukewarm attitude toward science, they acknowledge its importance in the curriculum, and dutifully teach the required concepts.

The majority of them follow the teachers' guide from 75% to 90% of the time, adding worksheets, films, speakers and magazines pertinent to the topics. Each grade level has a storage closet which contains the equipment needed for the science curriculum. The materials are arranged by units so that minimal time is required for maintaining or acquiring equipment. The district warehouse supplies the teachers with a few necessary components, but the majority of the consumable materials are purchased by the teachers on their own time. They are reimbursed from petty cash by the school secretary.

Although science is not textbook-based, students are still held accountable, as they are in all other subjects, for what they have learned and experienced. This insistence on accountability is seen by the principal as a distinguishing characteristic of the Perris faculty. Student achievement in science is generally based on three elements: participation, worksheets completed during a unit, and tests. There are no tests in the teachers' guides, so these are developed by the teachers. The fifth-grade team often utilizes open-note tests to ascertain whether or not the students understand the material.

This means of assessment is a sharp contrast to that of Western Elementary School, which is described below. Achievement of Perris students is reported to parents via letter grades, beginning in third grade. Minimal feedback is received from parents regarding science.

Western elementary

The students of Western Elementary School come from suburban middle class homes; the majority of them walk to and from school. The class size ranges from 25 to 30 students. The teachers are primarily middle-aged (35-50)—experienced teachers who have been with the district for 10 to 25 years. The majority of those years have been at Western, so there is a high degree of familiarity among the staff.

In spite of this positive picture of collegial relationships, there are few indications of teachers sharing insights they have discovered about teaching or about new techniques they have implemented in the classroom. Change appears to occur very slowly in this environment, and the principal is taking several steps to encourage professional growth in a supportive manner.

As in many schools, there is a substantial variance of teachers' instructional styles within the faculty at Western. The three particular teachers who were observed, however, consistently created child-centered, nurturing environments on the numerous occasions when they were observed.

The science curriculum is integrated with other subjects, particularly social studies and language arts, in the two third-grade classrooms. Integration is not viewed as the best practice by the district's science cadre, but the principal supports the teachers' decision to implement the district's program in the way they choose. The two teachers feel very strongly about the benefits of subject integration and would welcome a more in-depth examination of the practice by the district staff. As in the case of Perris, the teachers have considerable longevity in the district and the science curriculum is firmly entrenched in their minds. They spend 1 to 3 hours planning a unit before it commences, and then approximately 10 to 20 minutes daily preparing for each lesson. The third-grade teachers plan as a team, although actual implementation varies slightly due to individual preferences.

Storage is seen as the main problem in the science program. Increased enrollment has taken the classroom space where materials had previously been stored. Boxes of equipment are now squeezed into every possible corner. The teachers perceive that there is also a problem, generally just for new teachers, in knowing how to teach with live creatures. They view the in-service classes as the main vehicle through which teachers can initially become comfortable in dealing with animals.

The students at Western love science. As one teacher said, "They love the touching, and grabbing things, and looking at things, and examining, and sharing and talking. . . ." Most activities are small-group tasks and the students learn to listen and support one another. Four or five desks are grouped together to facilitate this sharing. At least half of the science class-period provides for active, direct student involvement with hands-on materials. Assessment of student achievement in science is generally based on attitude and effort, as well as on participation, and the written products completed during a unit.

Activity-Based Learning in Practice

The varied forms of elementary school science found in the Sheridan County schools are reflected in the practices of these two schools. While the district program largely determines the substance of science education, which leads to many similarities between Perris and Western, the manner in which the program is put into practice varies considerably between the two schools.

Contrasting approaches

Because the range of practices among Sheridan County elementary schools is fairly well represented by these two schools, the differences between them are informative.

- Teacher attitudes vary: Western teachers genuinely enjoy science and teaching it, while Perris teachers are not particularly fond of science but teach it to the best of their ability, given their interest in it.
- Instructional practices differ: Nearly all of the Perris classrooms are teacher-directed while the classes observed at Western are child-centered.
- The relationship between teacher and student is not the same: In most classes observed at Perris, teachers and students tend to interact in a formal, traditional manner, in contrast to the obvious warmth and high degree of comfort between teachers and students in classes observed at Western.
- The amount of subject integration is different: Very little subject integration occurs in grades 3 through 5 at Perris, but a great deal of integration occurs at Western, particularly in third grade.

• The methods of science assessment are not the same: grades and tests are stressed in the science classes at Perris, while participation, attitude, and effort are stressed at Western.

• The level of student involvement in science is different: At Perris, most students limit their interaction with scientific principles to science class and science-related homework. They do not appear to be absorbed by science; their approach is more passive. At Western, most students appear to "live science" throughout the day. They will stop to observe their "critters" and to make comments about scientific issues in the environment outside of science class. Their approach to science is more active.

The Western approach deserves more elaboration than given above. The children in these classrooms interact positively and comfortably with their peers and their teachers. The focus of each room's physical environment and of the activities within each room is clearly on the children's needs and interests based upon their developmental level. The students exhibit great enthusiasm for learning and are always anxious to share their discoveries with each other and with any adult who is present. The science curriculum is integrated with other subjects—particularly social studies and language arts—in the two third-grade classrooms. As mentioned above, integration is not viewed as the best practice by the district's science cadre—possibly because some teachers have used it as a way to reduce the time devoted to science—but the principal supports the teachers' decision to proceed as they choose.

Similarities

In spite of the differences in commitment to activity-based learning in science at Western and Perris as described above, there is a relatively high degree of similarity across the two schools in both the *teachers' overall mode of operation* when conducting science lessons and the *students' pattern of activity*. A typical science lesson consists of three distinct elements: (a) introduction, (b) active student involvement with materials, and (c) closure.

In a typical lesson, for approximately 50% of a class period students are actively involved with science materials. These materials may be objects such as microscopes, batteries, with bulbs; or they may be live creatures such as mealworms, crayfish, or crickets. During this portion of the lesson, the teacher walks around the room acting as a facilitator, as she interacts with individuals and/or small groups. Usually, the students are working on a project in pairs or in groups of four or five.

They utilize their observation and critical thinking skills as they experiment, alter various conditions, and record their discoveries. Talking and movement characterize this part of the lesson.

The district program

The science programs that exist in each of the dozens of elementary schools in the district reflect both the centralized program established by the district and the characteristics of each individual school. This is evident from the multi-faceted descriptions provided below.

Accessibility

The materials and support services which are the basis for this district program are readily accessible to teachers. Each one has a teachers' guide as well as ready access to supplemental guides for the various units. The district science support staff is viewed as highly accessible.

Practicality

Opinion among teachers varies about the practicality of the activities. The curriculum is sequentially organized. Several teachers would favor the use of materials found in the children's backyards. There is some disagreement about the openness of the curriculum to teacher choice and originality, although most teachers pick and choose the activities they think are best suited to their students. There is a wide variance in the number of teacher-designed original activities.

Curriculum fit

The science curriculum is an integral part of the district program and is firmly entrenched in the schools. District-wide curriculum goals are carefully stated in a way which has the science goals integrated into them. The expected learning outcomes are outlined at the beginning of each teachers' guide. These goals include general objectives for kindergarten through sixth grade, and grade-specific objectives as well. The teachers see the activity-based curriculum as a good contrast to their other curricular areas, which are less student-centered.

Instructional planning

The teachers perceive that most of the hard work of planning has been done by the district and provided to them in the form of the teachers' guide and the instructional materials needed for hands-on instruction. They feel that the amount of preparation they have to do is relatively small. The teachers welcome a thoroughly planned curriculum so they can spend more time planning reading and math activities.

Teachers describe the preparation time devoted to the science program in terms of two categories: unit preparation and daily-lesson preparation. When asked to describe the amount of time they devoted to preparation of a unit, common answers were "a couple of hours," "45 minutes plus" and "just the amount of time needed to pull the materials together." When asked to describe the amount of preparation time involved in daily lessons, the great majority of the teachers gave a response that fell somewhere within the range of 10 to 20 minutes.

Extent of use

The observed fourth- and fifth-grade teachers use from 75% to 90% of the activities in the guide. The observed third-grade teachers, on the other hand, selected from 25% to 50% of the activities, and in the remainder of the science time, supplemented the program with their own materials. The majority of teachers use at least 75% of the activities in the guide.

Cooperative planning

Cooperation among school personnel is valued by district leaders and is encouraged by such means as in-service training programs and support processes developed by the district. The form this cooperation takes could reasonably be expected to vary greatly from one school to another in a district as large as Sheridan County. The degree of cooperation at Perris and Western is relatively high, but this is confined to grade levels where teachers plan instruction together rather extensively.

Testing

The only district-wide testing in the field of science in Sheridan County schools is done with a test developed by the district itself. It contains items thought to be closely tied to their own curriculum. One of the aims is to have consistency between the curriculum and the test. Interviews with district staff do not leave the researchers with a strong impression that these tests are the most accurate measure of student achievement of curricular objectives; one gets the impression that the testing process was established more for the political purpose of maintaining the program within the existing social and educational context.

Nature of the Program

The district-wide Sheridan County science program has clearly become an integral part of the established order, but the nature of this established practice deserves further explication. The majority of the teachers adapt the curriculum in some way, but teach science within the suggested time frame. Activities are selected and modified according to teacher preference, student interest, and availability of materials. Although most teachers feel that they can adapt and select the most appropriate activities, they are using the district program largely as it was intended.

The commitment to activity-based learning in science among teachers takes varied forms. For example, in one sense the commitment at Perris Elementary School is very high. The hands-on program provided by the district is to a large extent the only thing the teachers know, and for the most part they assume—incorrectly—that other school districts have similar programs. In another sense, however, the commitment of Perris teachers to activity-based learning in science may be relatively low. For example, they are concerned about the lack of substantive content and supply such items as worksheets and closure activities, which emphasize the learning of very specific knowledge. Deep down, they are committed to a form of education which is more accurately reflected in other aspects of their curriculum, namely, one in which the emphasis is not on student activities and the processes involved, but upon specific knowledge outcomes which can be assessed by paper-and-pencil tests and demonstrated by students verbally. Thus, there is a tension between the program as they are expected to teach it and the deep-seated educational values of the majority of the staff of the school. The program succeeds not because it is totally consistent with teachers' personal values but because it is established and operated in a way that to some extent overrides these basic values.

In contrast, the observed teachers at Western appeared to have personal philosophies that were more congruent with the activity-based science program they were being asked to use. Tests were not used and teachers were much more interested in process—not just product.

In the context of this varied pattern of school practice, a significant question arises as to whether or not the instruction taking place in classrooms is of the desired nature. Are the activities being done for their own sake or as a vehicle for important science learning? The classroom observations were, of course, conducted for this purpose. In an effort to communicate more fully the findings of these observations, field notes were reviewed in detail at the end of the project to identify the different instructional approaches employed and to classify the teachers according to these approaches.

A Classification System

In doing this classification, a set of categories was used which was developed by Fleming (1990) for a study of activity-based elementary science. Her analysis of instruction in another setting yielded five major instructional patterns, which we have consolidated into four for our purposes, as follows.

The dubious type

Teachers of this type doubt that science is important for students at the elementary level and rarely teach it.

The "facts" type

This type of teacher focuses on science facts, vocabulary, and other specific information. When hands-on activities are used, they generally come after getting the information and are done according to specific procedures provided to the children.

The invitation/exploration type

With this type of teacher, students are introduced to a variety of phenomena and are given many opportunities to manipulate materials and explore on their own. The emphasis is on the experience and closure commonly is not pursued, even though the teacher wants the students to learn concepts.

The integrated type

While teachers of this type use exploration and invitation in science classes, along with explanation and applications of ideas, considerable emphasis is placed on students drawing their own conclusions and engaging in problem-solving skills. Science is seen as both a body of knowledge and a way of acquiring new knowledge.

Using this set of categories, the teachers from Western and Perris schools were classified. All of the teachers at Western were judged to be in the integrated category, while at Perris the teachers were classified as mostly in the facts category, with one each in the integrated and exploration categories.

Implications

To more fully understand these variations in teaching approach across the district and their implications for the type of science learning encountered by students, additional interviews were conducted with district personnel having in-depth knowledge of elementary science in the district. The interviews addressed questions such as these:

- To what extent are these schools typical of the district?
- Does the apparent relationship between teachers' style and the particular school in which they teach, if fact, exist across the district?
- What percentage of teachers, district-wide, would be found in each of the five categories?

Although this case study provides a limited basis for dealing with school effects within the district, there is a substantial basis for saying they exist. Coordinators of the various subject areas, such as language arts, math, science, and social studies, are said to compare notes occasionally and to comment on the similarity in instructional approaches across subjects within a particular school. Such information strengthens the inference that there is substantial variation from school to school, in spite of a district-wide curriculum and the many district strategies described earlier for implementing and maintaining the program.

Without question, the activity-based program is heavily used across the district. But it is of interest to know the extent to which it is used in the various ways described above. In order to better understand this, the above information was discussed in detail with the district coordinator of the elementary science program. With this program as a full-time responsibility, a role definition which puts her in schools for a large part of her working time, and with an in-depth understanding of elementary science education issues, she is in a position to offer an expert judgment as to the prevalence of the several types of instruction. After careful discussion of the situation—including discussion of data collected in empirical research studies and in observation records compiled over several years of conducting the Instructional Improvement Process in many schools—she offered the following percentages as an approximate indication of their prevalence:

Instructional Type	*% of Teachers*
The Dubious Type	5%
The Facts Type	15%
The Exploration/Investigation Type*	50%
The Integrated Type	30%

* Because the distinction between the invitation type and the exploration type was not always clear in our context, they were combined here.

She is of the persuasion that the exploration/invitation type could be thought of as the typical district teacher, even though the goals of the program and the efforts of its leaders are directed toward the integrated type. In this typical class, science is taught, it involves many activities, and students are excited about it. In such classes, the tendency is to assess students on the basis of their participation in the activities.

The History of Activity-Based Science in the District

Activity-based learning in science has a long history in the Sheridan County schools. District leaders with a long-term affiliation extending back over 30 years expressed the opinion that understanding the current program is not possible without going back in time—at least into the 1950s. It is said that the curriculum is the glue not only for keeping the science program in place but also for maintaining district instructional programs in general. In the early 1950s, the district adopted a *centralized* approach to the curriculum.

A second early characteristic was a philosophy of *innovation*. As the district moved into its second decade of existence in the 1960s, this philosophy of innovation is said to have been very prevalent. During the 1970s the district science program—originally developed in the 1960s—underwent a major revision which took several years to implement. In some cases, units of the science program retained much of what had been used in the past. In other cases, units underwent substantial revision, or were simply discarded and replaced with new ones. This revision is noteworthy for its exemplary implementation endeavors. The Concerns-Based Adoption Model (CBAM) (Hall & Loucks, 1978) provided the guiding principles for this endeavor. Careful attention was given to responding to teachers' needs at various stages of the implementation process. Thorough attention to the levels of use of the curriculum (as defined in the CBAM) characterized the endeavor, and its impact is still apparent today in that the levels-of-use terminology and operating principles are still evident in the instructional improvement endeavors undertaken by the district.

Examples of steps taken centrally by the District to address teachers' concerns and to attain an institutionalized program include provision, at no expense to individual school budgets, of all the materials and supplies needed to operate the science units during their first months of use. This approach is typical of the District curriculum development efforts; the acquisition of materials is not in any way left to chance at this point in the process. As a program shifts from the field-test stage to routine use, the responsibility for provision of such materials and supplies is shifted from the district level to the individual school. The district still maintains a warehouse of different kinds of materials, but each school must order such materials as needed, paying for them out of its own budget. The specific ways of managing the ordering and resupply process, and the means of organizing such materials and making them accessible to teachers in the school, is strictly a school-level responsibility. This situation relates closely to another factor, namely, the steps taken to provide training for principals. The intent is to engage them in a leadership approach that gives high priority to providing materials and other support within their own schools. In-service training was, and continues to be, provided for principals with respect not only to equipment-supply matters, but to the very philosophy and goals of the program, as well as to the means of providing the needed support and leadership to teachers.

Institutionalization

From these beginnings it is clear that the program moved on to become, in some sense of the word, institutionalized. Activity-based learning in science is assumed; it is "just the way it is done" in this district. Reported below are descriptions of various means of on-going support, and related conditions, that extend back in time quite a number of years.

Replenishing supplies. Even though it varies from school to school, each school has a system of replenishing supplies and materials needed for the district's hands-on science program. The manner in which it is to be done, however, is decided upon within each local school. According to district personnel this form of supply generally takes one of three forms:

1. Materials are organized in kits, one for each unit in the program. Each kit is complete, even though this arrangement may mean that a kit has duplicates of materials in another kit that is not being used at that time. The kits are contained in a locked storage room for which only one person has a key. This person is the one responsible for inventorying the materials and reordering expendable supplies as needed. A teacher can check out a kit through this person.

2. Under this system, the materials are organized item by item on shelves in a storeroom. When ready to teach a particular unit, the teacher turns in a list of items needed, and they are pulled off the shelves and assembled for the teacher's use. When the unit has been completed, the items are returned, inventoried and placed back on the shelves in their assigned locations.

3. Under this arrangement, the materials are maintained in kits, but the kits are stored in individual classrooms and each teacher (or sometimes a grade-level leader) is responsible for inventorying the items and reordering expendable materials as needed.

District-level personnel favor the first of these options, although the choice of a system is up to each school. Although the lack of easy access to the kits under the first option is distasteful to some teachers, district-level personnel are persuaded that this minor problem is more than offset by teachers' satisfaction with a dependable system that consistently gives them complete and ready-to-use kits. One opinion expressed by a district science-department staff member was that in all but five of the elementary schools in the district (about 6%) one of these options was in operation in a manner that could be said to handle the matter quite satisfactorily.

Administrator understanding and leadership. Resolution of the materials-supply problem depends upon local school leadership on the part of the principal. The in-service education provided for principals is designed to develop an understanding of what leadership is needed for the science program and provide the principals with such additional skills as are needed to carry out this role. This training is one of the means by which the district instills a commitment to a particular set of goals and provides principals with the skills needed to exercise competent leadership.

Training of new teachers. Each new elementary school teacher entering the Sheridan County School District receives 2 or 3 full days of in-service education related to the very specific science program they will teach. Typically, two in-service classes are conducted for each grade level, one in late September and one in late January. The workshops are conducted by two classroom teachers under the direction of a district science coordinator. Components of the in-service classes include:

- hands-on experience with equipment and live creatures;
- discussions about student learning;
- modeling of questioning strategies and procedures to use with students;
- sharing of experiences by attendees who have taught units;
- tips on management and organizational issues;
- the importance of utilizing cooperative groups;
- discussion of safety issues;
- availability of resources.

Training for teachers with new assignments. Any teacher shifting from teaching at a given grade level to some other grade level receives one day of in-service training related to the specific science units used at the new grade level. Such training is typically provided during the first month of the school year, on school time, with a substitute teacher provided.

No support for an alternative. No textbooks are provided for students in the area of science; they are simply unavailable, and no money is available for purchasing them. A textbook approach to teaching science is not an accepted alternative in the district and no support of any sort is provided which would aid a teacher in embarking independently on such an approach.

Activity-based learning in science is the norm. Hands-on science has become a part of the culture of the school, in the sense that it is the way everyone expects science to be done. To not teach science in this manner would go against the norms of the students, parents, and teachers. It may not be possible to delineate all the details of how this norm was established, but it is clear that training, the concerns-based adoption approach to innovation, and ongoing support are all part of the process.

Cadre staff. A so-called "Cadre Staff" of elementary teachers from across the district was established to provide assistance to schools needing help in implementing and sustaining their hands-on approach to science. Some of the assistance is provided on an on-call basis. A teacher or principal wanting assistance can contact a member of the Cadre Staff directly, but more often the contact is made by calling the district science office where someone in turn contacts a Cadre Staff member.

The more significant role of the Cadre Staff is to be a part of the systematic approach adopted by the science department quite a number of years back called the Instructional Improvement Process (IIP). This is a specific formal process under which one or more members of the district science staff and of the Cadre Staff work with the principal and teachers of a given school over a substantial portion of a school year to assist them in improving their science program. It is a carefully designed process in which these outside persons review the ongoing science program and compare current practices with 12 so-called "key features" of the science program to determine how well it is meeting district expectations.

Staff academy training. The Sheridan County School District has a very extensive ongoing program of in-service training for teachers, which is conducted under the name of the Staff Academy. Some courses are specifically designed for support of particular portions of the curriculum, such as the science in-service classes; others are of a more general nature and are open to teachers on an elective basis. Although the resources committed to maintaining this endeavor may seem large, given the above descriptions, the cost-per-pupil is relatively small. Now that the program is in place, it is estimated that the annual cost-per-pupil for centralized district support for science is approximately $2.00. This figure does not include the money spent for resupply of materials, which is part of the budget of each individual school. A rough estimate of the cost of resupplying these materials in the typical school is also approximately $2.00 per student per year.

In summary, it can be said that activity-based learning in science has been incorporated into the district program. It is reflected in broad goal statements, in the curriculum materials developed specifically for the district, and in the variety of means of ongoing support. It has become a part of the culture of the district; firm expectations and mechanisms are in place to provide for its continuation. A hands-on science program has not only been implemented, it has become institutionalized, and means have been provided for its maintenance.

Explaining Institutionalization

Teacher commitment to activity-based learning in science varies considerably. Teachers actively and willingly participate in the program and carry it out largely as intended. On the other hand, at some schools, there is little evidence that it has been incorporated into the teachers' own value systems or that they would make extensive efforts to maintain this sort of a program if the district support and guidance were not present. There are numerous indications that the basic values of many teachers are more closely congruent with the form of education employed in areas like writing, reading, and mathematics, where the approach is more textbook bound and tied closely to paper-and-pencil skills.

This situation also raises a very important question for researchers and policy makers. If this somewhat limited degree of commitment has been achieved in a situation where science is highly supported and valued, how much hope is there that activity-based science learning will emerge as a common form of instruction if left solely to teachers? The indicators of such a status are quite limited in the Sheridan County School District. On the other hand, one might argue that the highly centralized approach to curriculum used in the district is unlikely to generate this type of ownership. Is it not reasonable to expect that teachers who developed such a curriculum on their own would have a much higher degree of personal ownership and a more internalized commitment to teaching science in this manner? If the answer to this question is yes, one is still faced with the question of what curriculum development and implementation procedures can or should be used to engage teachers in such efforts with a reasonable expectation that such a commitment will emerge.

The questions raised above with respect to teacher commitment could also be addressed to school institutionalization. Since institutionalization in the school as a whole is largely a reflection of staff commitment, one is inclined to view institutionalization as being somewhat synonymous with the *teachers'* commitment. The degree of institutionalization at this overall school level may be considered somewhat higher, however, largely because of the important role and commitment of the *principals*. Possibly because of the strong district commitment to activity-based learning in science, and principals' view of their role in the district, there is reason to believe that the school-level commitment is somewhat higher than it is among the teachers in general. One is still left with the question, however, as to whether or not the principals' commitment is to this type of science learning per se or simply to whatever science program the district has and promotes.

Every indication is that district-level institutionalization is very high. It is reflected in district goal statements; policy decisions made by the Board of Education; administrative decisions made by central administrators at all levels; and the skilled actions of the science department staff with respect to program development, implementation, and program maintenance and support. District institutionalization is clearly present and the program is used throughout the district. This situation does not remove, of course, the questions raised earlier about the extent to which the district's ideal is reflected in teaching practices across the district and the means by which it could be further realized. Since in many school districts science is often not taught extensively (a reflection of the dubious type teacher?), and when taught, is usually taught by the facts type teacher, the long-term persistence of the district program as described above is clearly a major success story from the perspective of advocates of activity-based science programs.

But there are still questions for which answers would be helpful. Would it be possible to move even further toward integrated type instruction becoming predominant in the district? Given the variation in instructional approach among schools, is there a limit to what can be achieved with centralized district curriculum implementation? Or is this variation an indication that the centralized process can not go further without moving to a more intensive and extensive process of working with principals to enhance their involvement in the process of providing the leadership for the desired form of instruction within their buildings? Is the increased interest in site-based management today (not just nationally, but in this district as well) an opportunity for moving toward an even better science program in the schools? Or will it be the cause of erosion and a slide away from the level of excellence currently in place?

Why has this institutionalization occurred?

The long-term experience of the Sheridan County School District clearly establishes that a district-wide activity-based science program can be institutionalized on a large scale. Given the relative rarity of such occurrences among school districts, however, a high priority question is: how has it been accomplished? This question has been at the forefront of the researchers' minds and has been reflected in the information sought from district personnel in interviews. A variety of factors are involved, of course, and it is of interest to know what they are, their relative importance, and the ways in which they can interact.

Commitment. The major reason for institutionalization advanced by the person in charge of the district's science program is consistent with other information and judgments developed through this case study: the first priority factor is that of commitment to having activity-based learning in science, and a commitment to taking whatever steps—within reason—are needed to bring it about. This commitment has a long history and is present at the highest levels (i.e., the Board of Education and the Superintendent). It has been present for several decades. Leaders are committed to activity-based learning in science and are committed to those processes needed to implement the commitment.

Institutionalization expertise. A second important factor in the Sheridan County situation is the expertise among the science department staff with respect to curriculum implementation. They not only understand the process of development but the process of implementing and maintaining a program with integrity. It is a systemic view that does not treat development as the responsibility of one group of people and implementation as the responsibility of another.

Effective implementation strategies. A natural outgrowth of expertise is the utilization of a process having true integrity. In this instance, the Concerns-Based Adoption Model (CBAM)of implementation has had a prominent role. Attention has been given to the relevant concerns of teachers at various stages of the process. Attention has also been given to the CBAM to levels of use and to the measures that need to be taken to achieve full implementation with integrity.

In-service education. Yet another outgrowth of the previously identified commitment and expertise is the in-service education program operated by the district through its Staff Academy. This has not been in-service education for its own sake, but in-service education designed to be part of a larger systemic effort to achieve the desired implementation.

Support staff. Another form of program support is direct attention to teacher concerns. This support is exemplified by the Instructional Improvement Process and the provision of the Cadre Staff to assist teachers as needed. A proactive stance is taken with respect to instructional improvement. Mechanisms have been developed to monitor science instruction and to assist teachers, as needed, to utilize activity-based learning in science with integrity.

Replenishing supplies. The provision of needed supplies for doing hands-on science has often been identified as a crucial matter. Again as a result of district commitment and expertise, this problem has been fully addressed.

Other. Other specific matters (e.g., the arrival of new teachers in the district each year and the need for periodic updating of some units in the program) could be identified and described in some detail here. But as in the earlier cases, the answer is really in the commitment and expertise referred to earlier.

Chapter 8

Patterns and Examples of Activity-Based Learning in Practice

A profile of instruction in the 15 IMPACT schools was developed to portray patterns found across several schools and to provide examples of specific practices. As stated in chapter 2, our main interest is in the activity-based learning processes employed in teaching science. In order to analyze the patterns in the varied and voluminous case descriptions, we adapted the conceptual framework of Klein (1991, pp. 24-41) who suggests categories for analyzing curricular processes and decision-making. For our purposes we reduced her list of nine distinct curriculum elements to the following five broad ones:

- learning and teaching activities;
- content;
- materials and resources;
- time and space;
- evaluation.

We subsumed Klein's element "goals, objectives, purposes" into other categories, especially "content," and the element "grouping" into "learning and teaching activities."

Under each of the five headings we present general patterns in our cases, including major variations. Although the emphasis in our selected cases is on successful practices, we refer also to some problematic issues, as well as to the kinds of solutions that were tried.

The descriptions of general patterns are supplemented with specific examples from individual cases (approaches, events, utterances of participants) in order to illuminate the findings. Sometimes some our own reflective comments and conclusions are added.

Learning and Teaching Activities

In the initial stage of our work, before starting the case studies, we developed a portrait of "ideal" practice in activity-based learning having the following characteristics (Hameyer et al. 1988, p. 33; see also chapter 2):

1. The pupils develop their own ideas for inquiries, experiments, or constructive work. They search for explorative methods to clarify and illuminate questions they consider meaningful.
2. Students investigate meaningful questions or problems on the basis of their own ideas. They explore their ideas and apply various methods.
3. Students analyze, discuss, and evaluate what they have found or constructed; they display their results in the classroom or elsewhere.
4. Students express their understanding of what they have learned. They exchange findings or constructive results, and they draw conclusions where possible or appropriate.

This characterization reflects the central value that is attached in this approach to an active student role in the learning process. For this reason, it makes sense to start with a description of the functioning of the students themselves. Then we will proceed with the salient features of the teachers' activity patterns and the quality of the learning environment.

Student Involvement

A dominant pattern in our cases is a *high level of student involvement and enthusiasm*. The children like activity-based approaches very much, especially hands-on and outdoor activities, including opportunities to learn by doing and by engaging in independent work.

This level of involvement was not only evident in the numerous lessons observed but could also be inferred from the remarkably strong retention by the students of activities carried out months earlier. This phenomenon was particularly apparent in some of the German IMPACT schools (e.g., Schwanensee, Foerdeschule, and Heideschule).

Student Initiative

The degree of student initiative in the learning process grew substantially in the latter years of our studies, but was generally not as strong as described in our characterization of ideal practice. Examples of assertive student initiative were most apparent in the Swedish cases Asken and Granen, and in nearly all German cases. This high level of student initiative in planning and conducting activities seems to be strongly supported by *weekly- or daily-plan teaching* in schools where students are given a significant degree of personal choice in what to do during a week. In this open-education approach, the students have, besides a common core of instruction, a considerable amount of time on their own during lessons for personally developed individual work. Teachers of some schools (e.g., Stadtparkschule and Birkenwaldschule) reported that this approach tends to foster process and inquiry skills such as planning, observation, problem solving, and communication, and that it stimulates a capability for self-regulation in the learning process.

Instructional Pattern

In all schools, a shift has occurred from a direct pattern of teaching toward more group work. Cooperative activities are common, some of them in mixed-age groups. In general, the level of interaction (both teacher-student and student-student) is very high. Whole-class events are usually concentrated in the beginning and final stages of lessons. A typical pattern (of a rather structured approach within the possible range of activity-based strategies) may be found in the Sheridan County case (U.S.A.).

1. *Introduction*: review of previous lesson(s) and learning; overview of the day's activities; content instruction; directions for the day's procedures; answers to students' questions; set-up and distribution of learning materials;

2. *Active student involvement with materials*: students usually work in small groups, while the teacher plays a facilitating role;

3. *Closure*: discussion of what was observed, attempted, and learned; student sharing of products; highlights of upcoming activities; clean-up and collection of materials.

Profiles of less structured activity-based approaches, with more opportunity for students to make decisions about what they want to investigate, can be found in some of the Swedish and German IMPACT schools discussed earlier. A valid conclusion for all cases is that the teaching approach equals a stimulation-and-facilitation type, as opposed to an information-transmission-style.

Variation in Resources and Experiences

The more active kind of learning also implies an increased variety of resources—materials and objects—that students may use, and of the sorts of experiences in which students engage. This variety of resources and experiences may be relatively prestructured through instructional materials—as in some of the Dutch and certainly in most of the U.S. cases—or be stimulated by the open learning environments and pedagogical approaches found in most of the German and Swedish cases. Outdoor activities and excursions have also become a more or less regular part of the learning experience in many cases (e.g., Meerzicht, Schwanensee, Heideschule, and Shadow Crest).

Variation Between Teachers

Although the general trend toward an activity-based learning approach is recognizable in all cases, there is a rather wide variation in the beliefs, and especially in the practices, of the teachers involved. These differences are present not only among but also within individual schools. In most schools, teachers vary considerably in the stage, scope, and depth of their involvement in the changes under way. In several cases (e.g., Meerzicht, Linden, Stadtparkschule, and Shadow Crest) there seems to be a gap between "forerunners" and the majority of the teaching staff. And in some schools (e.g., Spruce) the trend toward innovation seems rather superficial; there are not sufficient changes in the actual behavior and beliefs of the teachers to speak of really successful institutionalization.

Typical Problems

As in all serious innovative efforts, the implementation of activity-based learning is not without problems. Typical problems include the barriers identified in the Dutch cases:

- the conceptual and organizational complexity of the teacher's role (e.g., dealing with unanticipated student questions; diagnosing learning problems in matters where the teachers themselves sometimes do not feel very confident; and maintaining a balance between autonomous student initiatives, small group activities, whole class events, and structured lessons);
- time-consuming lesson preparation;
- difficulties in evaluating learning outcomes.

Simple solutions are not evident. In the case of Veldwijk, the teachers tend to put some restrictions on the number of topics they introduce to the students. This approach widens the opportunity for quality learning by way of comparing and discussing findings, while limiting the time invested in preparing and evaluating instruction. "Less is more" seems to be the premise behind this approach.

CONTENT

Common to all cases is the *integrated-curriculum pattern* embodied in the activity-based approach. Three methods of integration may be discerned. The most modest is to integrate subjects such as biology, physics, and chemistry into "science education" or "inquiring nature" (Regenboog, Meerzicht, Spruce, Shadow Crest, Sheridan County, Valley). In these cases, the biology component is usually the most prominent. The second method of integration is to integrate natural and social studies, as in *Sachunterricht* in Germany, *umvärldorientering* in Sweden, and *wereldoriëntatie* in the Netherlands, (see Veldwijk, Asken, Schwanensee, Foerdeschule, Stadtparkschule, Heideschule, Birkenwaldschule). The third and most commonly used method of integration is a general approach of activity-based learning that permeates almost all instructional processes and curricular content in the school (Granen, Linden, Foerdeschule, and Birkenwaldschule).

Another common feature in our cases is the extensive integration of topics with project-oriented activities. These activities are often spread over a long period, sometimes months. The original planning for such activities is usually done by the teacher, but there is wide variation in the degree of student influence on the coverage of the topics, the use of resources, and the character of the discovery and inquiry activities.

In most cases, a lot of emphasis is put on *process skills* for exploration, *learning to learn*, and on such attitudinal goals as *curiosity*, *exactness*, and *perseverance*. This emphasis does not mean that content goals are unimportant, but content is probably less in the forefront than in more traditional approaches.

As may be expected from the different kinds of integrated offerings, the scope of content varies widely across cases. While the following list of topics is far from exhaustive, it illustrates the variety of themes observed in lessons among the 9- to 10-year-old children:

- heartbeat and respiration;
- propagation of humans, plants, and animals;
- the construction of towers;
- trees around the school building;
- making sounds;
- the behavior of dogs;

- the functioning of cars;
- the human body;
- how to measure temperature;
- electricity;
- stars;
- environmental pollution;
- water;
- animals with coats;
- bacteria;
- beans;
- newspapers;
- traffic;
- the protection of nature;
- exploring natural phenomena downtown;
- space;
- earth science;
- whales;
- rocks and minerals;
- the properties of snow;
- soil.

Materials and Resources

Variety is the key word for describing the materials and resources actually used in activity-based learning. In contrast with more traditional methods of teaching science, *the textbook has lost its prevalent role.* Only in two of our cases—Shadow Crest and Valley—are textbooks used as an instructional tool. Even in these schools, textbooks are not the single source of information and action; they are combined with other instructional materials such as kits and media.

The most frequently used aids are various types of instructional materials, often a combination of guidebooks for the teachers and work sheets for the students. These materials are developed externally as much as internally. Also common is the "documentation center," a media area or recreational corner in the classroom which offers many kinds of background information, activity incentives, learning resources, games, and books for further reading.

Many schools, especially the European ones, have a school curriculum that describes the goals, content, and methods of instruction at the schools. In many cases this specification of general curricular frames or guidelines is at a national or state level. These school curricula tend to have little influence on daily instructional practice, in which instructional materials are much more powerful.

In the U.S. cases, many curricular decisions are made at the school-district level. These decisions strongly influence teaching practice because the supply of materials (teachers' guides and kits) and other support, such as consultant services or in-service training, are usually linked to the district curriculum. A good example of such highly structured and comprehensive policies is described in the Spruce case:

- The district science curriculum states general goals and describes 28 units (four per grade level).
- Each unit comes with a teachers' guide that includes an overview of the unit, background information for the teacher, and sequential activities.
- Each activity includes objectives, process skills, a materials list, procedures, suggested questions for discussion, student activity sheets, and suggestions for extending the activity.
- Teachers are provided with one kit per unit, which contains all the materials, handouts, and equipment needed to teach that unit.
- The kits include various items such as posters, videotapes, filmstrips and evaluation measures appropriate to the unit.
- Each teacher receives a kit from the district's science center four times during the school year. (The kits are resupplied with materials at the science center. They are delivered and returned on a district-wide mail truck.)
- A corresponding principals' guide addresses the supervising task of the principal.
- Each teacher attends an in-service class, conducted by the district's science consultant, on each unit before it is taught for the first time.

A nice example of school-based materials development is described in the Stadtparkschule case. In Stadtparkschule, the teachers themselves produce the majority of their own teaching materials and prototype equipment. Topics are discussed and decided upon at the beginning of and during the school year; ideas for teaching-games are exchanged and developed. The games are often such that the pupils are able to discover or make up their own rules. The teachers use a wide variety of materials, including games, textbooks, flash cards, work sheets, LEGO sets, cut-out systems for personal testing, building sets, technical models, equipment for experiments, plasticine, printing sets, personal newspapers, and documents. An interesting detail is that most materials and games follow a self-instructional educational design, which enables the pupils to check their own work and to see what the next steps are. Thus, they do not depend so much on the teacher's advice and help in order to resolve problems.

Another example of internal material provision is given in the Veldwijk case. Over the course of several years, the teachers at Veldwijk have built up a large stock of written lesson ideas. All the materials are stored in a file, with a reference system to facilitate retrieval.

TIME AND SPACE

It is hardly possible to estimate reliably the amount of time that teachers in our cases spend on activity-based teaching and learning in science. It is difficult because of the various degrees of integration of science content (as described earlier) that blur time boundaries. Moreover, most teachers use a rather varied time allocation. Not only are there often regular times scheduled for specific science education, *Sachunterricht*, etc., but time-consuming projects are also frequently planned, in which students work on comprehensive themes for extended periods on various occasions and at irregular intervals. For many of the German and Swedish schools this approach is typical, especially in those schools using daily or weekly plans.

In cases with a clearly defined science subject the average amount of time scheduled for science varies considerably—about 1 hour per week in two Dutch cases, and about 1.5 to 2 hours in the U.S. cases. The estimated figures for the German cases are comparable to the Dutch practice, or even below, as *Sachunterricht* with its 3 to 4 lessons per week covers a lot of other topics and subjects (for further detail see chapter 5).

To what degree is the activity-based approach also visible in the learning environment? It appears that in five of the cases (Asken, Granen, Schwanensee, Stadtparkschule and Birkenwaldschule) the classrooms clearly reflect this approach. They do not have rich natural environments or a lot of space in the school buildings (although such favorable conditions may exist, as in the case of Meerzicht), but they have accomplished a purposeful redesigning of their classrooms. In some classrooms of the Schwanensee school, for example, different zones have been created for reading, building, construction, and cookery. There are also special learning zones with carpets and armchairs, an exhibition area, and many kinds of bulletin boards. The walls are decorated with pupils' work and the tables are distributed in various arrangements.

Another example of this is found in Stadtparkschule. The tables constitute several working areas for groups of students, complemented with a communication zone for all. Library and learning-material shelves serve as semi-transparent room dividers. Equipment is readily available, a sitting and theater corner has been established, and side tables are available for exhibition purposes and for displaying students' work. Some zones are carpeted. The whole learning environment is inviting, friendly, comfortable, and readily adaptable to many arrangements. Yet another example of excellent facilities and a positive learning environment can be found in Birkenwaldschule (see chapter 5).

Frequently mentioned in our cases are the special provisions and the time required of personnel to store and maintain all the materials, equipment, and other resources in an accessible and efficient way. It is a matter of high importance and is handled in different ways in the various cases.

Evaluation

The teachers in our cases almost unanimously report a very positive impact of the activity-based approach on the students (see the section on student involvement). Most of our classroom observations support this conclusion—especially concerning the enthusiasm of the students—but of course these data are impressionistic and do not provide measures of ultimate learning outcomes.

Many teachers express a positive opinion about the progress of students. For example, in the Stadtparkschule case the following claims are made:

"The pupils like the new kind of learning. Many can hardly imagine traditional classroom teaching. Their social achievement and ability to co-operate have noticeably increased, especially the ability to direct the work themselves, to do joint work, to look for and find information, to make decisions with others and implement them. Their ability to concentrate and their motivation to learn are results of the weekly plan (i.e. no chaotic behavior, quite the contrary)."

In most cases there were no signs of systematic attention to the assessment of learning outcomes. Evaluative activities are usually done during closing sessions with the entire class, when experiences, findings, and products are shared and discussed. The evaluation of individual progress and achievements is mostly rather informal. Student effort is often seen as top priority; more formal assessment of learning outcomes is not very common.

There are some cases where at least some effort is made to monitor the progress of pupils. For example, in the case of Veldwijk, teachers have developed registration sheets for that purpose, and teachers at

Valley tend to use so-called "application-level assessment kits," with an emphasis on observation and on the grading of products.

The general impression is that evaluation and assessment receive little systematic attention, although the schools seem to vary in their concern about it. Some perceive it as an important but difficult problem, so they want to pay more attention to it; others feel no need to invest more in this matter and thus seem not to care about it.

Chapter 9

Explaining Institutionalization: Cross-Site Analysis

Each of the schools making the journey toward activity-based learning principles has its own history. Most of the schools which make up our 15 cases have reached a "mature" level, but some have stopped at an earlier level or are still in process. We have tried to map out these histories using concepts common in research concerning improvement

FIGURE 9-1
A Redesigned Learning Environment

processes in schools (Miles & Ekholm, 1985). The change from traditional teaching to activity-based learning principles in science has been viewed as a process that moves from the initiation of working methods to a period of implementation and reaches fruition with the institutionalization of the new orientation.

Initiation is the stage in which new ideas are proposed, commitment is sought, and the local organization begins moving. Such initiation activities are common at the beginning, but they also occur throughout the entire improvement process as more and more portions of the organization move in the new direction. During the implementation stage, new ideas, procedures, and activities are put into practice; the new orientation is tested in relation to the old classroom patterns. If the new and the old can work at the same time, institutionalization may result. If they cannot coexist, a struggle between the new and the old begins. If the new wins out, institutionalization has occurred. This subprocess of institutionalization has been a primary focus in the IMPACT project; it involves a change being stabilized in the system's internal structure in such a way that it will endure after the improvement effort is "over" (Miles, 1983).

The three subprocesses mentioned—initiation, implementation and institutionalization—are closely related to one another and often overlap. It is often difficult to distinguish them from each other in schools being studied. In spite of the hazy boundaries between these stages, the three concepts have been helpful in understanding the improvement processes that we have traced backwards in time. An overview of these stages in the 15 cases is presented in figure 9.2 and is elaborated in the remainder of this chapter.

The Initiation Phase

Interviews with staff members of the schools concerning their schools' histories show initiation periods varying in length between half a year and 3 full years. Only half a year were used for the initiation process by the two Dutch schools participating in the project work with activity-based learning as its core. In the German schools a year was taken in three out of four schools. In the three Swedish schools and four American schools initiation ranged from 1 to 3 years.

The length of the initiation process seems to depend, among other factors, on the ways in which the school year is organized and on the manner in which activity-based principles were introduced to the school. The short initiation period in the Dutch schools, for example,

FIGURE 9-2
Overview of the Development Process of the Schools

SCHOOL	INITIATION	IMPLEMENTATION	INSTITUTIONALIZATION
Schwanenseeschule (Germany)	Two teachers started. Individual need to enrich own teaching practice. Internal support by principal. Initiative in line with renewed educational policy. Duration about 1 year.	Took about 2 years. Several teachers tried the new in their own way and tempo. Step-by-step progress. Continued exchange and cooperation with parents. Redesigning classroom as activating learning environments.	Continuously linking progress with renewed educational policy of state. In place after 3 years. 4 out of 10 teachers are users. Steady effective informal and practical support by administration. Congruent development of school and administrative policy.
Heideschule (Germany)	Principal initiated and provided exemplary practices and ideas. In-service education of the teachers and solicitation of involvement of the teachers. Duration 1 to 2 years.	Took 2 to 3 years. The principal intensified his initiatives on what he was good at—project-oriented activities, particularly in environmental studies. Development of materials and ideas for instructional choices. Step-by-step progress with strong advocacy by principal and indirectly by students' enthusiasm.	In place after 4 or 5 years. The principal is steady in continued school improvement, encouraging more staff members to participate in the new. Publishing curriculum materials. Linking with in-service education. Participating in a newspaper project which helps the school to disseminate its findings and expertise.
Foerdeschule (Germany)	Started by principal who stimulated other staff members by doing the new himself. Clarifying benefit of activity-based materials	Principal who is strongly accepted as a good teacher continues over 2 years, gradually gaining other staff members who explore the	Half the staff is using activity-based teaching practices by now. The school is on its way to institutionalizing the working pattern.

Continued on next page

FIGURE 9-2 *(continued)*

SCHOOL	INITIATION	IMPLEMENTATION	INSTITUTIONALIZATION
	and its acceptance by students, providing ideas, materials and resources.	new. Preparing a resource center for curriculum materials. Commitment and practice evolve step-by-step.	The school does not focus on disseminating its working pattern to other schools.
Stadtparkschule (Germany)	Teachers took initiative. Support from principal. Innovation in line with reshaped policy. Practical reason was to create a better childhood at school. Dissatisfaction with conventional teaching.	Cooperative school climate and institutional identity. Elaborated culture of school-based feedback and sharing of ideas. Working with individualized materials. Redesigning classroom learning environment. Effective cooperative climate among all staff.	Students' progress and increased learning motivation inspires continuity. Sharing with other schools. School visits and embedding the new in in-service education. Video about new practices at Stadtparkschule produced. Parental involvement.
Birkenwaldschule (Germany)	Responding to changed childhood circumstances, student learning habits and experiential knowledge. Impetus from resource center in the school called *Lernwerkstatt* (Freinet Pedagogy.) Dissatisfaction with conventional teaching. Educating for personal and social development, curiosity and taking responsibility for one's own learning.	Developing open teaching methods and choices for students' participation in learning activities. Strong links to community. Securing accessibility to new practices for other schools and in-service education.	Sharing of common educational principles by all staff members. Securing commitment of new teachers joining Birkenwaldschule. Exchanging with other schools regularly about progress of innovation. Completely reorganized classrooms, activating learning environments.

Continued on next page

FIGURE 9-2 *(continued)*

SCHOOL	INITIATION	IMPLEMENTATION	INSTITUTIONALIZATION
Regenboog (The Netherlands)	School accepted invitation to participate in national project emphasizing activity-based science. Principal strongly in favor and all teachers supported it. Stimulation by attending regional conference and visits of curriculum developer. Initiation took a couple of months.	Took about 2 years. Curriculum materials used according to plan. External support by developer for individuals and pairs of teachers (classroom observation and feedback). Meetings to discuss experiences. Cooperative planning and reflection by pairs of teachers. Principal was effective internal facilitator. Agreements written in school work-plan.	The program is in full action in the third year. External support has stopped. Principal still active as facilitator, especially regarding materials and other resources. He monitors progress and problems in staff meetings. Teachers encouraged to articulate their own approaches and develop their own plans. A couple more years of experience needed for secure institutionalization.
Meerzicht (The Netherlands)	School accepted invitation to participate in national project emphasizing activity-based science. Teachers liked concrete nature of the innovation. Project conference offered stimulating and instructive start. Initiation took a couple of months.	Took about 2 years. Major input through monthly staff meetings with discussion and reflection on work. External curriculum developer introduced new ideas and materials and coached teachers (including classroom observation and feedback). Teachers inspired by regional meetings with teachers from other schools. Planning for activity-based science themes.	External assistance stops after 2 years. Pedagogical approach of activity-based learning firmly rooted in school, but individual teachers face problems in time planning. Coordination of individual and common decision-making rather weak, which hinders stabilization of the new approach in the regular working pattern. Some external support still seems desirable.

Continued on next page

FIGURE 9-2 *(continued)*

SCHOOL	INITIATION	IMPLEMENTATION	INSTITUTIONALIZATION
Veldwijk (The Netherlands)	Twenty-year tradition with *Jenaplan*. Prior training on educational change. Assistant principal skilled as change agent and advocate of activity-based learning. Started four-year project on "world orientation" (natural and social sciences). Had helpful external advisor.	Took about 3 years. Elaborate planning by assistant principal and external advisor; plan followed. Monthly teacher meetings to discuss ideas and exchange experiences. Teachers try new ideas and materials. Assistant principal offers individual assistance and coaching. Educational advisor supervises team process. Principal supportive and focuses on organizational management.	Fourth project year aimed at consolidation; emphasis on longitudinal planning. Completion of three practical publications. Activity-based approach continues in fifth year as regular pattern, and broadens to other subjects. Continuous fine tuning in sixth year as another "world orientation" project is started to improve content structure and activity planning.
Granen (Sweden)	In *kommun* where school is situated, central administrator arranged in mid-eighties for a specific school to use activity-based learning as its central focus. Principal was recruited with special interest in activity-based learning and teachers selected on same basis.	Principal and teachers used planning time before school was built to plan the new working plan for daily life of school. From the beginning of the school these methods have been in use together with other working patterns.	Activity-based learning patterns are part of school from its beginning and is institutionalized then. It took many years before the school was built to "muddle through" the idea of a separate activity-based school in the *kommun*. The central administrative body and some teachers were behind the process.

Continued on next page

FIGURE 9-2 *(continued)*

SCHOOL	INITIATION	IMPLEMENTATION	INSTITUTIONALIZATION
Asken (Sweden)	Teachers and principal seek new educational approaches in mid-eighties because of difficult backgrounds of students. Principal initiates multigrade teaching. Teachers discuss new approaches for a year before starting first use.	Multigrade teaching is introduced over a 3-More teachers became interested in activity-based learning after the first two teachers had used the new working pattern for a couple years. But it took four years before some opponents of the new approaches had left the school and several other teachers began participating in implementing the new patterns.	After more than 4 years activity-based learning is institutionalized. Several teachers use it, but it is intimately linked to the use of multigrade teaching. It is used as a tool for individualization within multigrade parts of school. The teachers travel to other schools to disseminate their working pattern through in-service education events.
Linden (Sweden)	One teacher started new educational approach and several years later another teacher joined in. One teacher longed for omväxling and needed to change her pattern of work with the children.	More teachers became interested in activity-based learning after the first two teachers had used the new working pattern for a couple of years. But it took 4 years before some opponenets of the new approaches had left the school and several other teachers began participating in implementing the new patterns.	After 6 to 7 years, activity-based learning and other changes became "invisible." Multigrade teaching helped stabilize the new working pattern. School leaders supported the development. New central guidelines highly favored activity-based learning. The new managerial structure of the school, where the local school got more power, supported the dissemination of the new working pattern in the school.

Continued on next page

FIGURE 9-2 *(continued)*

SCHOOL	INITIATION	IMPLEMENTATION	INSTITUTIONALIZATION
Sheridan County (United States)	Under a supportive school board and administration, science supervisor begins developing activity-based science program including curriculum guides for teachers and manipulative science materials for students. In-service education for teachers and principals, systems for supplying materials, and other support are developed.	Teachers from all schools are provided with needed materials, in-service education and assistance. Teacher concerns are systematically identified and addressed. Principals are given in-service education on how to foster improved instruction and resupply materials. A science Cadre Team supports individual teachers and conducts review of program in schools	No other form of science taught in the schools. Means of maintaining program are institutionalized in the district, including: in-service education for new teachers and those changing grade level; science cadre; systems of resupplying materials; and a systematic instructional improvement process.
Valley (United States)	District administrators develop activity-based science program including teachers' guides and kits of manipulative materials to be distributed to schools as needed from central supply center. Teachers play key role in designing activities and testing them with children.	Teachers receive inservice education, get kits they order, and participate in developing additional instructional kits. District administration promotes program and includes science in outcomes assessment process the district is developing. Implementation extends over 3 years.	Program is the standard working pattern for many teachers and is approaching institutionalization, but is not yet at that point.

Continued on next page

FIGURE 9-2 *(continued)*

SCHOOL	INITIATION	IMPLEMENTATION	INSTITUTIONALIZATION
Shadow Crest (United States)	"Leadership for change" characterized both district and school. District policy is activity-based science but schools implement policy. Principal promoted collegial grade-level teams and appointed a science committee to plan curricular change. Committee developed kit-based plan. One teacher prepared kits during summer.	District had science in-service education but not focused on curriculum. Teachers learned by teaching the new materials. Collaboration with peers in teams was most important in learning new approaches. Principal promoted new forms of pedagogy (e.g., cooperative learning).	After 5 years activity-based science program is widely used in school, but new pedagogical practices have not been extended in a major way into other parts of curriculum. Principal is attempting to expand collegiality and foster further pedagogical change in the school.
Spruce (United States)	District appointed supervisor to develop hands-on science program for their seven schools. Program based on teachers' guide and kits of materials was developed. Kits were mostly adapted from ones available from other sources. Supervisor did the most development with some teacher input.	Teachers introduced to program unit by unit through in-service education programs. Kits of materials provided to teachers. A principals' guide was also developed. Students have high interest in the science program, which has influenced its acceptance.	Three years after program began it is institutionalized. Teachers in this school are enthusiastic supporters of the program. It is sustained by the help of the supervisor, in-service education, and provision of needed materials. Acceptance of program is related to its quality, flexible structure, hands-on approach, student interest and learning, and opportunity for teacher modification.

seems to be a result of a message received by the schools in the spring that they had an opportunity to participate in the new science project. The schools quickly reached their decision to participate in the project and work started that autumn.

The 3 years that initiation took in one of the Swedish schools is related to the way in which that school is structured; the teachers follow a class of students for 3 years and then start with another group of students. The start of a new working pattern there was combined with the teachers' reception of new students. The teacher who started the innovation in this school used activity-based learning for 3 years; in the meantime other teachers studied her experiences so that they were prepared to start the new patterns of education as they received a new round of students.

In one of the other Swedish schools, innovation began when the school switched over to non-graded teaching as a result of a decreasing number of students; when one change was made another could follow readily at the same time.

In one of the German schools, Heideschule, a new principal brought ideas about activity-based learning with him, and had to promote the ideas repeatedly over a school year. He had to acquaint teachers with both himself and the new ideas at the same time. In this school and in some of the other German schools, the principals themselves taught children in this innovative manner, and thus shared with teachers both the problems and the problem-solving tasks.

One of the American schools is situated in a school district where, when the district administration attempted to persuade the local schools to adopt activity-based learning in science, the staff in the school responded positively to the challenge. It took a couple of years before the materials were widely used in the district, and this followed in-service education sessions where explanations were given about how schools could work with activity-based learning.

THE IMPLEMENTATION PHASE

The crucial part of the improvement process seems to be the implementation phase, when the new is tested by the teachers in the school and is critically evaluated by others—such as the school board, parents and, perhaps most importantly, the students. For a new working pattern to grow in a school and become an integral part of that school's daily life, all—or at least the most powerful of the actors—must accept and like the replacement of old patterns.

In the schools we have studied, implementation of activity-based learning depends a great deal on one or several teachers becoming enthusiastic about the new working pattern. The presence of a kind of "bridge-leader" in the school, permits other factors to have a supportive or determining influence in the European schools.

In three of the five German schools, initiation of the new practice began with two teachers who cooperated closely with each other. In two out of three Swedish schools, an individual teacher initiated the new practice in the school. In each of the U.S. schools, initiation of the new practice began with individuals other than teachers. In three U.S. schools the initiative came from district-level personnel and in the fourth one a new principal brought the ideas into the school. In these schools teachers accepted the ideas for improvement and infused them into their own working pattern. In two of the three Dutch schools, the teachers as a collective unit choose to test a new practice.

It is not only the American schools, however, where the district or local school administrators are active in getting activity-based learning into practice. In the American cases the school leaders were the initiators. In most of the European cases, the teachers took the initiative with the explicit support of their school leaders. But in several European cases, school leaders or central authorities *were* initiators.

In two of the five German cases, for example, it was the school leader who took the initiative to use activity-based principles, and in one German case the teacher initiative had strong backup support from the school leader. In one of the Dutch schools a new assistant principal came onto the scene and revitalized the working pattern of the school. In one of the Swedish cases, the local board of education decided to create a model school based on activity-based learning. They appointed a school leader whose task it was to establish activity-based learning as a central working method of the school. In the other two Swedish cases, the school leaders were very supportive of the initiation of activity-based learning.

Upon analyzing the reasons that activity-based learning was introduced in these schools, several cases were seen in which teachers' motivation for change was based on changes in students' family and community circumstances. In two German schools, conditions changed as more immigrants and more children with separated parents appeared at the school. The change in family and community conditions (die veränderte Kinderheit) was also important in the other German schools, but was not consciously perceived there as it was in the first two mentioned.

In all three Swedish schools the students were organized in nongraded classes, with a wide age span among the students, creating a need for more individualized and independent working methods. In two German and two Swedish cases, teachers pursued changes in working methods together with the students as a result of their own feeling of a need for change, or as the Swedes call it, for *omväxling* in their work.

Implementation of activity-based learning in the 15 schools has generally taken 2 to 3 years. In the two exceptions, implementation took place more quickly. In one Swedish school and in one American school, it took only 1 year to implement the idea of activity-based learning.

Differences in the Depth of Use of Activity-Based Learning When It Has Been Institutionalized

The 15 cases of activity-based learning in science that we studied differ in the depth of their use of the pedagogical principles. Most of the schools (10 out of 15) are mature users of activity-based learning. In these schools, the approach has been in use for several years and is no longer challenged. Activity-based learning in science is present in the other 5 schools but is still some distance from reaching its full potential.

In two instances (Valley and Schwanenseeschule) use of activity-based learning principles had passed through the initiation and implementation periods and was approaching institutionalization; activity-based learning there could be characterized as stable. In three schools (de Noor, Reuter and Shadow Crest) we entered at a rather early moment in the historical process of integrating activity-based learning principles into the school. Implementation of the new approach is on its way, but it is too early to talk about an institutionalized working pattern. In our work we have termed them as "fresh" relative to the use of activity-based learning principles.

In these three schools, use of activity-based learning is clearly restricted to science class periods. In one of them, use of activity-based principles is found only in Grade 4. This situation is apparently similar to the way some of our more stable and mature schools performed in the early years of their innovation process. Innovation typically begins in a small part of the school organization, and in some cases stays in this small area over the years. In other cases, activity-based learning principles spread to other areas of the school. In some schools, activity-based learning began in subject areas other than science and spread to science after some time.

The new pattern is well accepted today in the mature schools. The working pattern of students pursuing investigations on their own is seldom challenged. Teachers as well as parents accept that "this is the way we work in this school." Schools we happened to study rather early in the process of innovation report more challenges (e.g., in one of the Dutch schools). Teachers say that the activity-based learning principle threatens old working habits that are rather economical to use. They may also perceive the activity-based learning approach as only one possible choice among competing "new" working methods they are not yet really sure about.

In the mature schools where activity-based learning is firmly established, our interviews show that this took from 3 to 8 years, with 5 to 7 years being most common. The shortest period of institutionalization, 3 years, was found in a German school, and the longest period, 8 years, in an American school. In the two schools where the innovation had most recently become a stable part of school life, it had taken 3 or 4 years.

Coincident Development

Upon studying the learning processes in these schools, we found, in addition to the expected activity-based learning, other changes in traditional school patterns. In several schools, for example, teachers were working in teams, and the work followed rather flexible time schedules. These apparently coincidental improvements or changes do not seem at all coincidental when analyzing the cases. In many cases, important interactions among several factors underlay the challenging improvements—such as activity-based learning—that were institutionalized in a school. It does not seem to be enough to get teachers to taste the use of activity-based learning. Most teachers know something of this principle and its practice, but they do not use it in a stable and routine way unless several conditions are present.

Social pressure

One of these conditions seems to be the influence of other people, especially those in leadership positions. It may be the district administrators, as in the case of Western and Perris in the Sheridan County School District in the U.S. In the case of the new Granen school in Sweden, the local board of education decided on the new educational approach and appointed a school leader to create a totally new unit of this type in the *kommun*. In Heideschule in Germany, the local school leader encouraged and stimulated his teachers to do the same. He acted as pilot and explorer to his teachers and hoped others would follow.

These influences may also come from the teachers themselves rather than from the formal leaders. At Schwanenseeschule and Stadtparkschule in Germany, teachers found that they needed to change the working pattern because students coming to the school did not respond to their teaching as previous students had. The students had different habits, due to different home conditions. More of these students were restless and had difficulty concentrating when traditional teacher-dominated work was assigned. Activity-based learning was seen as an alternative way to tackle the problem of motivating the students. When teachers started to change, they conveyed the expectation that their colleagues would do likewise. The same social pressure seemed to exist in the Dutch school, Meerzicht, the Swedish schools Linden and Asken, and the American school Shadow Crest.

Origins of the change

The findings from our study illustrate two distinct ways in which schools came to use activity-based learning. In the Netherlands and the United States, it had its roots in concerns about the quality of science teaching. In Germany and Sweden the activity-based learning pattern grew from more general educational changes encompassing all subjects, and was particularized in science.

Flexibility and materials may help

In our investigations, we looked for organizational and material conditions that could explain why the new approaches became a stable part of the school's working pattern. In addition to the important factor of teachers working well together and being organized into working teams, flexibility in the way that time is budgeted in the school appears to be important. In some schools (e.g., the Swedish schools and the German Stadtparkschule) large blocks of working time are put together, which helps teachers direct the students in individual investigations that take more than one or two lesson periods to complete. In other schools, such a change seems to be a major break with the school's traditions, and it helped to reserve special lessons for the use of activity-based learning. As a result, it became something that was "legal" to do in the school.

In most of the schools (12 out of 15) the presence of learning materials designed for this activity-based teaching approach was important for its institutionalization. This condition was not necessary in all the contexts we studied, as several of the schools altered their working patterns without such specific materials. Teachers in the three Swedish schools, for example, created learning materials together with their students as they utilized the new principles.

In some schools a component of the whole working pattern seems to involve students making their own learning materials. Birkenwaldschule in Germany, has its own printing office where products are made. The Shadow Crest school in the United States has produced material kits that others use. The provision of specially designed learning materials supports the institutionalization of activity-based learning. It seems to be a positive step towards initial use of activity-based learning principles in many kinds of schools. In some contexts, such as in the schools of the Sheridan County School District in the United States, supplying such materials was crucial in achieving institutionalization on a mass basis in dozens of schools. In other cases, it appears that the type of activity-based science learning being pursued did not demand certain materials, and/or the teachers were more open to preparing their own learning materials because of personal outlook or because of the availability of time and other resources.

Composition of classes

The manner in which students are grouped seems to be important in some schools, both for initiating and for institutionalizing activity-based learning. In the Dutch school, Veldwijk, and in the three Swedish schools, the students are not grouped in classes strictly on the basis of their age. The non-graded strategy used in these schools demands that the teachers individualize student learning. And it also makes it necessary to individualize the treatment of groups of students in the same class, where the groups contain students of different ages and knowledge backgrounds. With its strong profile of student initiative and production, activity-based learning has been one possible solution to the problem of how to assist students in a differential manner.

To own the new pattern

The long-term and steady use of activity-based learning found in our investigations is also partially explained by conditions other than the ways in which students are grouped, how teachers work cooperatively, or the presence of learning materials. To persist as a natural component of a school, activity-based learning must be "owned" by the staff of the school, or at least by some parts of the staff. The degree of ownership varies in our schools. For example, in one of them, Granen in Sweden, the whole staff is appointed on the basis of a positive attitude towards the use of activity-based learning.

In several other schools, such as Birkenwaldschule, Linden and Veldwijk, the whole staff seems to own the ideas, and over the years such opposition as once existed has been fading away. In two of these schools, old opponents of the new approach have left the school and new opponents have not been appointed. In schools with rather homogeneous attitudes among the staff, it may be easier for activity-based learning to last for many years to come, as compared to schools, where the working climate allows more choice of working methods among the teachers. This statement is speculative, in that some of the schools adopting activity-based learning over the long term have made the working pattern a natural part of the school's inner life, even though there is not universal ownership of the idea. In these schools only some of the teachers or school leaders have a strong feeling of ownership of the working pattern, but this seems to be enough to maintain the pattern in the school over a long period of time, even though the working pattern is fully institutionalized only in a portion of the school.

Whether ownership of the activity-based learning principle is collective or individual, it is probably a mirror of the climate of the local school. Some schools have developed a strong degree of collectivism and of collaborative working relationships. Teachers work in teams, with each one having different tasks and responsibilities. School leaders direct their work towards collective groups of teachers; they do not turn to individual teachers. In other schools, the basis of the work climate is more solitary; each teacher acts as an individual and has his or her well-defined work area, where people have little or no input. We found variations on this solitary/collective dimension among our 15 schools; the working pattern of activity-based learning has been institutionalized in variations all along this dimension.

In-service education

To grow, activity-based learning needs "food." In the schools we studied, this was supplied through in-service teacher education. In several schools, in-service education programs, such as study days, courses, or reflective meetings, are held on the theme of activity-based learning. Teachers report that through in-service education they get acquainted with kits of materials, new experiences, and fresh ideas of how to use activity-based learning. In-service education of teachers, in connection with the initiation, implementation and institutionalization of activity-based learning in science, is found in all the schools we studied. In-service education focused on activity-based learning has been one of the key factors in the development process in these schools.

Staff stability

Maintaining activity-based learning in a school is certainly facilitated by stability among the teaching staff. Since it takes a long time for activity-based learning to become embedded in school life, advocates of this working pattern must persist in their efforts over a period of years. In some schools, the motivators are teachers who have been using the new approach since its introduction into the school. In other cases, school leaders continue over time to support and push for activity-based learning. For more than a decade in the Sheridan County School District the science department staff continuously supported the new orientation in many ways in their contacts with teachers. In the Veldwijk school, the assistant principal, supported by the principal, actively pushed the teachers for more than 7 years to take responsibility for being a *Jenaplan* school and to use activity-based learning principles.

Dissemination as a spur

In some of the schools we noted an aspect of dissemination that was a strong influence on institutionalization. Birkenwaldschule in Germany, de Noor in the Netherlands, and Granen in Sweden are all open to visitors from other schools who are interested in seeing with their own eyes how activity-based-learning is used in practice. These schools—and some other schools where activity-based learning teachers act as in-service teachers for other educators—seem to stabilize use of the new working pattern by spreading the message to others. It appears that schools where the teachers attempt to spread the new ideas to others are schools where the teachers must take seriously the consequences of what they are advocating. The school personnel seem to reason that if they are advocating the new method, they must continue its practice, so that there is no dissonance between their advocacy and their actions. This behavior of some of the schools, teachers, and school leaders creates a "good circle" in the lives of the schools. The interest of other schools in the practice rewards the staff members and encourages them to continue it. To be the focus of others' interest stimulates the preservation of the activity others want to study. Classrooms in Birkenwaldschule, for example, need to be full of the activity-based learning materials and student work that have attracted new groups of teachers to visit the school.

Rewards

This reward that some of the schools seem to experience from the interest of others does not exist in all the schools, and we have looked for other kinds of rewards that may have influenced stabilization of the new approach. No particular rewards stand out. The incentives found in the four different nations are of a discrete nature. Teachers, as well as school leaders, most often describe the reward found in the joy that students show when working in this manner. People also commonly feel rewarded when school leaders or colleagues exhibit the work of a teacher and his or her class and tell others about it.

Outside legitimization

To be labelled as institutionalized, a new working process needs not only to be legitimized by power holders within the school, but also by those outside the school. Inside the school, activity-based learning has been legitimized when it is accepted definitively by the people using it and is so well integrated into the users' value system that they identify themselves, in a conscious or unconscious way, with the practiced principle. Outside the school, legitimization is indicated when the power holders integrate it into the total gestalt of the educational system. As this happens, the power holders outside the school will be prepared to fight for the existence of the specific working pattern of the school. The identity of Birkenwaldschule as a resistant cell opposed to traditional distribution-like pedagogy, for example, was supported by the local school board, which demonstrates the legitimization of the working process of that school. The same message was signaled by the local school board in one of the Swedish *kommuns*, when it invited the visiting minister of education to Granen to look at the flagship of that *kommun*.

Few conflicts

We see institutionalization as a nonlinear process. No single standardized flow of events in the schools has fit activity-based science learning into existing local cultures. The schools' developmental histories differ and grow out of local conditions. When development occurs in local organizations, it is common to find dialectical tensions, gradual shifts in position, and conflict among different parties involved in the development. In our interviews, we searched for these phenomena, but did not always find them. In some schools, the local culture of the school minimizes conflict by valuing pluralism and accepting differences in working patterns among various parties.

Other schools that show signs of tension during the process of institutionalization, such as Granen and Linden schools in Sweden, experience pressure from outside, not from inside the school. In both of these cases, schools that students attend in their later schooling have criticized the previous schools' activity-based learning patterns as soft and too weak in their demands upon students. Rumors have also been spread that the later performance of these students is not as good as that of students from other schools. No hard evidence has been produced to support these rumors, however, but tension between these schools and their receiving schools has been evident. One effect of the tension between schools seems to have been an increased commitment to the ideas of non-graded teaching and activity-based learning principles in the criticized schools. The criticism has strengthened the schools' commitment to institutionalizing activity-based learning patterns.

A Long-term Perspective

The IMPACT study has taken a long-term perspective on change in schools. Studies of much shorter perspective dominated the literature about 20 years ago. Gross, et al. (1971), for instance, studied the initiation period of an innovation in a school district. Schmuck, et al. (1975) followed some schools through the initiation and implementation stages of an improvement endeavor. As a result of these and other short-term studies the interest of researchers and school-change agents was focused on the early and more manageable part of a longer development process. Gradually, interest in longer time perspectives has grown among researchers, which has fostered the construction of more stable concepts which are more helpful in understanding and managing improvement processes in schools.

With this longer time perspective in the studies has come more interest in the internal processes of change. This is seen in Huberman and Miles' study (1984) of 12 American schools engaged in improvement during the late seventies; in the study by Ekholm (1987) of 35 schools that tried to improve their lives in the early 1980s in Sweden; and in Pettigrew's (1985) 8-year study of organizational development strategies at Imperial Chemical Industries in the United Kingdom. The IMPACT study has looked at 15 examples of institutionalized activity-based learning to understand if researchers' notions about the long-term processes of improvement work can be trusted. We have found the concepts of initiation, implementation, and institutionalization to be useful. We have also seen, among other matters, that the slow-going, long-term process of development in schools is easier if teachers own the improvement and school administrators push for the changes to occur. The lessons learned in this study can be expressed as recommendations to other people who want to establish activity-based learning in their schools; these recommendations are the subject of the next chapter.

Chapter 10

Reflections and Recommendations

This final chapter builds on the cross-site analysis presented in the previous chapter; it provides recommendations gained from reflecting on the complete set of 15 case studies conducted in the four countries. Four of the 15 cases are found in this book (chapters 4 through 7) and illustrate the diversity of cases, but this diversity, of course, is even greater than seen in those four examples. Although the recommendations grow out of consideration of all 15 cases, each recommendation is obviously not reflected in all cases. Similarly, all of our recommendations do not fit every context where someone may think to apply them.

We recognize the fallacy of attempting to squeeze practical advice out of research data by deductive methods; the structure of scientific knowledge and the logic of practical reasoning (Schwab, 1978) are in principle incongruent. Therefore, our assertions have a note of tentativeness, even though they are anchored in common insights drawn from the cross-site analysis of all cases. Each recommendation will be specified and discussed without claiming complete adaptability in all countries or situations.

We believe these recommendations address the challenges elementary schools are currently facing, and help identify productive ideas for improving schools; we hope they help the reader reflect on alternatives. In offering these recommendations, we follow the assertion of Shymansky and Kyle that research should be more diligently applied to educational reform; that is, research should unify—not separate—the work of educational theorizing and practice (Shymansky & Kyle, 1991, p. 15).

Our recommendations are formulated for various readers: policymakers, support personnel, principals, teachers, and researchers.

Readers can also assess the cogency of these reflections and recommendations in light of their own readings of the four cases presented earlier, or of the full set of 15 cases presented in our extended report (cf. Ekholm, Hameyer, Akker & Anderson, 1994). The recommendations are grouped as follows:

1. Activity-Based Learning: Starting up—The Initiation Process
2. School-Based Self-Renewal: Going Further—The Implementation Process
3. Towards Routine: Anchoring the New—The Institutionalization Process

Each of the three groups of recommendations contains portions addressed to school personnel, such as teachers and principals, and portions addressed to those outside the school, such as support personnel, administrators, and policy-makers.

Activity-Based Learning: Starting Up—The Initiation Process

School Personnel	*Administrators Support Personnel Policy-makers*
• Start with what is familiar	• Clarify needs and choices
• Explore the new cooperatively	• Make a long-term commitment
• Integrate outdoor learning	
• Develop leadership	
• Facilitate self-renewal	

Start with the familiar

Innovations such as activity-based learning need to grow inside the school; repeated adjustment and adaptation is necessary (Sarason, 1971). At the same time, activity-based learning does not imply a complete change in a teacher's working habits. Activity-based instruction enriches learning opportunities. It can be learned and added to a teacher's repertoire without giving up valuable, established routines. If activity-based instruction is completely new, of course, it means a step into unknown terrain. We found that productive schools not only protect such expeditions into undiscovered land, but also explicitly support such tentative excursions as a preliminary step toward extended use.

In the German and Dutch cases, the "explorers" cooperated with experienced practitioners of activity-based learning as comrades-in-arms; on-site professionalism, experiential knowledge, and imaginative creativity were evident in an interdependent manner. Most innovative teachers in our IMPACT schools were not outsiders in their schools but were recognized by their peers as highly qualified teaching personnel.

Explore the new cooperatively

Teachers—along with principals—should create opportunities for learning from each other. Such opportunities are particularly important when activity-based learning practices are the goal; their implications for one's own teaching practice can be explored, learned, and adapted especially well in a collaborative context.

The getting-acquainted process should be protected against any pressure to commit to it from the beginning. The German and Dutch cases emphasize the hazards of pressing for commitment to new educational ideas. But if the staff is given sufficient time to get acquainted with the new approaches, to experience their benefits with children in the classroom, and to share experiences about good and bad aspects of the program with other teachers before additional steps are taken toward commitment, then the initiative is more likely to gain partners and develop ownership. Among steps that can be taken to foster this exploration are the following:

- provide for co-teaching in your school;
- encourage mutual instructional visits;
- develop instructional design ideas and materials;
- create site-based development efforts.

Integrate outdoor activities

Certain norms seem to be common in schools where activity-based learning is positively received. One such norm pertains to where the learning takes place. Experiential learning and exploring nature almost demand learning activities outside the school—in the biotopes or in the community. It is important that principals encourage teachers to:

- widen the span of experiential learning opportunities inside and outside the classroom;
- reorganize and enrich the classroom environment with more direct and frequent access to learning equipment; space for doing experiments;

and various activity areas where the students can construct things, play with others, cooperate on projects, and read;

- make outdoor learning an integral part of teaching and learning science (e.g., through caring for a biotope; observing birds on the school ground; doing environmental studies; and interviewing experts about puzzling phenomena).

Make a long-term commitment

Early in the development process, policy-makers and administrators need to prepare plans for the long-term; this is essential if the new venture is to succeed. From the beginning, there is a need to look ahead further than 1 or 2 years and to address the forms of maintenance that an activity-based science program requires. If the program is to become institutionalized, ongoing support will be needed, including, of course, the equipment and supplies needed on an ongoing basis.

Develop leadership

Continued leadership is essential for any long-term endeavor. In addition to making informed decisions and allocating needed resources, the leadership role requires fostering public ownership of decisions and supporting personnel in their work. Just as teachers need in-service education, support people and policy-makers need education concerning the new approach under consideration (i.e., activity-based learning in science, both before they make initial decisions about it and as they continue the process of developing the program).

Facilitate self-renewal

If activity-based learning is to be introduced in a school, renewal must take place. Our cases show that schools can greatly extend their capacity for self-renewal if policy-makers set clear goals and show that local creativity and innovativeness is strongly appreciated. Policy-makers must indicate from the beginning the aims and principles of any school-improvement process. This requires a clear vision and checkpoints along the road. The schools also need policies that are clear as to the degree of local responsibility desired and the degree of independence that is officially guaranteed. The freedom of local choices and district or national comprehensive policies should reflect a fruitful interplay.

SCHOOL-BASED SELF-RENEWAL: GOING FURTHER—THE IMPLEMENTATION PROCESS

School and Project Personnel

- Develop realistic time schedules
- Maintain step-by-step progress
- Ensure reflective feedback
- Foster stable collaboration
- Promote self-directed learning
- Explore the new by staff development
- Enrich the learning environment
- Combine with site-based development
- Diversify the learning environment

Administrators
Support Personnel
Policy-makers

- Support local choices and actions
- Inquire about educational progress
- Monitor the costs
- Provide materials and equipment
- Evaluate the new

Develop realistic time schedules

A realistic time schedule recognizes that any serious innovation effort usually takes 2 to 3 years to implement partially. In most of our cases the efforts continued for 4 to 6 years before they were anchored in the routine life of the school. Realistic time schedules should be set and agreed upon from the beginning to insure sustained professional progress, repeated feedback, and mutual learning about the new approaches; as well as incorporation into individuals' personal work patterns, open communication, and realistic expectations inside and outside the school.

In our cases, the school improvement process includes three interrelated stages: (1) developing the initiative, (2) implementing the new approaches, and (3) incorporating the new approaches into the routines and culture of the school (i.e., institutionalizing the new approaches). In all the IMPACT schools, successful improvement required personal and institutional commitment over the entire time span, from the initial effort through the final stage of the improvement being anchored in the school. The overall time schedule should clarify responsibilities, allow for developing shared internal and external commitment, and identify a vision of desired outcomes. People who are merely fascinated for a few weeks but not really committed to continued cooperative work are counterproductive.

Building a vision of quality science teaching, trying it out, being an advocate for it, maintaining professional curiosity, working to anchor the new vision in the life of one's own class and school, acquiring external support, and exhibiting exemplary practices are all actions that demand a plan with a clearly defined time schedule. The intent of such a plan is to reconstruct traditional work patterns to incorporate new approaches; active self-renewal should grow and flourish (cf. Caldwell & Spinks, 1988; Hameyer, 1993).

Our advice is to translate your conceptual framework for activity-based science teaching from the beginning into a long-term time schedule which fosters the reflective commitment of all participants. Then more specific actions in a specific time frame can be anchored into this general plan, such as integrating into the weekly schedule a 2- or 3-hour block of time during which a room is given to all staff for experimental work beyond the formal curriculum.

Retain step-by-step progress

School improvement is a socially complex process which follows spirals of progress rather than the logic of linearity. Evolutionary planning (Louis & Miles, 1990) is needed. Even if limited to two or three classrooms in a school, the change efforts are embedded in a system which, in turn, has to adapt to the new events. Therefore it is necessary to proceed step by step and to adjust the new to accommodate it to its environment. Short but consistent steps forward are more likely to succeed than are power-coercive models which push the new forward rather than creating change cooperatively. The following actions, among others, are central to such step-by-step improvement:

- Provide repeated opportunities and time for everyone to become familiar with the new approaches to teaching and learning.
- Clarify at each stage of the process what developments will come with that stage and what their impact will be.
- Encourage everyone to link the new approaches to their own current practices.
- Discuss and specify those current practices that should be retained.
- Discourage unrealistic expectations.
- Utilize experiential knowledge already gained at your school during earlier attempts to innovate; integrate the various change efforts in the innovation biography of your school (cf. Fullan, 1991).
- Try out the new without demanding premature long-term commitment.

Because improvement emerges gradually rather than appearing at a specific point in time, the people involved need room for tryouts, interim reflections, revising their preliminary thoughts about the new, looking at exemplary practices elsewhere, and other exploratory actions; everyone needs space—physical, cognitive and emotional—for their reflective learning efforts. For example, in several of the IMPACT schools, provisions were made for teachers to become familiar with—and to experiment personally with—the new approaches without being pressured for a commitment before getting a clear picture of their benefits.

Ensure reflective feedback

An important key to progress is a culture of feedback. When people do not clearly see the advantages of the new approaches or how to use them, they need an opportunity to express their concerns and to get repeated feedback from experienced colleagues or experts. At the same time, those who have already mastered aspects of the new should be sensitive to reservations some of their colleagues still have. Authentic communication promotes not only confidence but mutual learning.

In schools we studied, principals and other administrative stakeholders focused on continuing staff receptiveness to new ideas. They encouraged the giving and receiving of feedback about each step taken; this was considered most important.

Reflective feedback gives the benefit of innovation visibility and clarifies the nature of the innovation for everyone. Feedback provides constructive criticism from the outset and fosters transparency among the staff. The teachers of Schwanenseeschule and Stadtparkschule, for example, made their classroom practices visible and open for reaction both from their colleagues and from parents whom they invited to visit and even share classroom tasks. Thus, parents could look at the quality of instruction and at the effects of activity-based teaching on their children. The children's enthusiasm became evident, and parents could respond easily to what they had seen. In two of the Dutch cases, the teachers endorsed activity-based science learning because it was both very attractive and instructive for their children. Such feedback, in turn, strengthens the engagement and motivation to continue. Among other steps a principal can take to ensure feedback are:

- Ask for external advice, help and support from parents, as well as others.
- Share her or his thoughts about the innovation with all staff in regular meetings and conferences.
- Organize workshops and school-based development efforts to encourage new practices cooperatively, without forcing them.

• Provide for the innovators in the school to share their experiences with others.

• Avoid elite circles.

• Make feedback an integral part of organizational development in the school.

• Encourage mutual consultation and build tandems of innovative and more traditional teachers.

• Encourage the staff to visit classes where activity-based learning is already in place.

• Negotiate with the teachers about their in-service training time to use at least part of it observing existing practices of activity-based learning in their school or in neighborhood schools.

• Acquire personal knowledge by observing such practices at your school or other places and share your insights about them with others on a continuing basis.

Inquire about educational progress

Encourage local support people and inquire about the progress they have already attained. Local support experts and principals need to know that their efforts are highly valued by external stakeholders. They need to know that activity-based learning in science is viewed as an important component of the core curriculum. Asking questions of this kind is part of an interactive feedback paradigm which, among other things, should:

• enable school leaders and policy-makers to ascertain if sufficient attention is being given to such matters as teacher involvement;

• ensure that sufficient opportunities are provided for teacher involvement in planning, curriculum and instructional development, and collaboration with other teachers;

• encourage teachers' ownership of the new approaches, a matter that is crucial to their implementation.

Foster stable collaboration and collegiality

Sustained creative collaboration is a key to success. Working in isolation is most ineffective because it provides neither feedback to assist in correcting problems that arise nor encouragement in times of trouble. As a principal, support such initiatives in your school and prevent pioneer innovators from struggling alone; solitary efforts have a low probability of prevailing. To enrich the quality of instruction through activity-based learning, you can:

- establish cooperative links among colleagues who have innovative ideas;
- identify common tasks to pursue;
- show that your idea is not the only way to achieve the new goals (be curious about alternatives);
- explore and elaborate new ideas for implementation within small groups before advocating them more broadly.

Address the costs

Estimate the cost—long-term as well as short-term—before beginning or expanding implementation of the new approaches. Do not proceed with changes unless the key leaders and policy makers are firmly committed to it and have allocated the necessary resources for a *long enough period of time* that institutionalization of the change is likely to occur. Activity-based patterns of instruction are not institutionalized quickly. Beginning the multi-year process without a commitment of appropriate resources is unwise.

Promote self-directed learning

Most schools we studied, such as the Dutch Regenboog, the German Birkenwaldschule, or Linden and Granen in Sweden, incorporate activity-based patterns of science teaching with other practices derived from other foundational educational principles. Self-directed learning is a substantial and important example. Students are given a regular time of the week for independent activities of their own choosing. This pedagogical practice—particularly stressed in the Swedish and German cases—provides a strong incentive for the students themselves to take the initiative for learning. The students are then more likely to develop intrinsic motivation and engage in creative explorations.

Available and varied facilities such as easy-to-use materials and equipment, educational games, various activity sheets, activity cards for ecological inquiries, and other items, support this educational effort. Students are given direct access to them in the classroom and can easily use them according to their individual interests. This availability of stimulating learning aids in the classroom fosters a stimulating learning environment and is a prerequisite for active student involvement in scientific inquiry. In the schools just mentioned, instruction is based less on schoolbooks than it was 10 years ago; the classroom environment is more attractive, and methods are substantially child-centered. A wide variety of hands-on materials are stored in classrooms and made available to students in a completely unstructured manner. It is difficult to translate this approach into a few specific recommendations. Some examples are offered, however, for consideration within the reader's own specific context.

- As a reflective teacher, try out different types of activity-based learning methods and materials. Help the students do their own experiments and encourage them to explore nature both in school and at home. Allocate sufficient time and space for students to explore and do investigative studies. Teach them using a variety of information resources. Project work is often an appropriate and valuable method.
- As a school leader, develop good examples of activity-based practices and make them accessible to your staff. Show specifically how basic educational aims are supported and learning enriched by activity-based patterns of science teaching.
- As a collegial teacher or school leader, provide insights for others into how students work in an activity-based way. Share problems of implementing activity-based science teaching and practical solutions to such problems.

Self-directed learning is not necessarily limited to project work or to other methods such as weekly-plan teaching (*Wochenplan*). We discovered a kind of multi-method sandwich in our cases. Discovery learning, group work, debates and class discussions, presentation methods, and individual instruction build the daily practice profile in a vast array of combinations in these classrooms.

Explore new approaches through staff development

The German and Dutch cases emphasize that pressuring people to adopt a new method is counterproductive. Yet, if sufficient time is allowed to get acquainted with the new approach; taste it; share implementation experiences before next steps are taken; discover the meaningfulness of the new practice prior to any request for commitment; then you are more likely to gain partners and develop ownership. Specific steps in this direction include the following:

- Increase co-teaching.
- Organize mutual links among teachers and students of different classes (i.e., build partnerships among classes).
- Participate in site-based curriculum development.
- Allocate regular times for developing the innovation further and exchanging experiences about problems and progress.

FIGURE 10-1
Activity Schedule for the Day (Daily Plan)

• Use time as a collaborating teacher to participate in both the planning and implementation of activity-based learning in the school.

• Draw findings from reports and research studies about activity-based learning and discuss these understandings in in-service education courses, during study days, and in other types of school-based staff development.

Enrich the learning environment

What influences those who alter their teaching? We did not probe deeply into individual motives, but it is certain that many want their teaching job to be more fascinating. *Omvaxling* is the key word to note from the Swedish studies—doing work in a different way and changing prevailing roles and routines. This is an important motivator for change in many of the IMPACT cases (cf. Fraser, 1986; 1988; Wallrabenstein, 1991). Another motive is the desire for new learning conditions in schools and for changes in a person's working environment. In the restructured classroom environments of our cases children enjoy learning more. Restructured classrooms contribute to the well-being of children at school and foster direct experiential learning. One teacher said that she usually became exhausted easily, but she can spend the whole day in the changed learning environment where various activities were offered because the new way of teaching is so much more fun.

The arguments in favor of such reorganized classrooms and their invigorating learning environments are widely recognized. Schools can compensate to some extent for deprived areas of life and lack of out-of-school experiences by changing classrooms into more ecologically stimulating learning environments favorable to the development of children. Children learn more if they like going to the place of learning. Such classes are often substantially redesigned to offer more choice of activities through such means as group tables; a discussion area; library shelves and counters with learning materials as room dividers; apparatus which is freely accessible; a sitting and drama corner; and side tables for exhibitions and project results. Some zones in classrooms are carpeted; the result is a learning environment that is welcoming, friendly, cozy and varied.

In the history of education, people such as Parkhurst (U.S.A.), Petersen (Germany), and Freinet (France) have pointed out the link between the learning environment and learning outcomes. They stress that feeling at ease is basic for productive teaching and learning. Much earlier, Pestalozzi fostered the image of the coziness of a school "living room." Workshops, school gardens, kitchens, and ateliers—today often called "learning studios"—played a decisive role.

Support local choices and initiatives

Trust-building between policy-makers and school personnel is central to enduring self-renewal. Authorities, support experts, administrators, and policy-makers are expected to back local decision-making for school improvement. Schools need timely clarity about external support, including its quantity and quality and its relationship to assured local responsibility. During implementation, administrators and policy-makers should facilitate the process of identifying:

- the overall needs for creative school improvement;
- educational values to be pursued;
- needed conditions and funds for support;
- innovative choices of high priority;
- visions of the desired profile of the school;

• structures for a reflective interplay among the various spheres of school improvement (i.e., the school, its district, the policy makers, support agencies, in-service education providers, administrative decision units, and research institutions).

They should also provide:

• encouragement for risk-taking efforts;

• a system of identifying and publicizing exemplary practices and projects which solve current vital educational challenges;

• programs for school leader education which foster cooperative organizational development;

• a clear policy of support for productive schools;

• programs for school-based staff development and school renewal (e.g., study days in Sweden, when the school closes once a year for a week of school-based review activities and planning for the coming year—a system which has been a routine nationwide practice there for more than 30 years);

• means of developing public and professional awareness about productive schools, whether by a report series, by setting up partnerships among schools, by launching a computer-based communication system or other appropriate means of communication among schools of different districts or regions;

• a competition in which schools are invited to present their best examples of activity-based learning, with the best examples published in a journal and presented during an exhibition where a prize is presented in view of the mass media.

Provide materials and other equipment

The provision of equipment and materials needs close attention in activity-based science teaching. There are many means of provision, but however it is done, someone must attend to it diligently. The case studies showed instances of it being addressed at the district level, within individual schools, and even by individual teachers. The district-wide systems in the United States provide one example of how materials can be made accessible across a number of schools, although it is also recognized that different approaches are viable in other educational settings. Although most school districts in the United States do not have such district-wide systems, the following examples from our cases illustrate the range of approaches that can be used.

In one system, the equipment and materials for the various activities are organized into kits pertaining to specific facets of the curriculum. These materials are housed in a central district building where a staff person handles orders for the kits, resupplies expendables and missing or broken items upon return of the kits, and revises the kits as needed to better fit the curriculum. The kits are distributed to schools and returned to the central location via the district delivery system that makes daily deliveries and pickups at all buildings.

In another system, equipment and materials are the responsibility of each school, but the district supports the schools by providing in-service education for principals as to various ways of dealing with the matter at the building level, and by maintaining a district warehouse of materials. Different building-level approaches have been used, including the following: (1) Kits of materials for each curriculum unit are provided for each teacher to keep in his or her classroom (materials are immediately available as needed by the teacher, but there is a greater cost than with some other systems due to the duplication of materials in several classrooms); (2) Kits of materials are provided for each curriculum unit, but they are stored in a central location within the building. There is a check-out system and some person such as a teacher's aid, a teacher, or even the principal, is responsible for keeping the kits restocked and for managing the check-out system; (3) The materials are stored centrally in the building, but rather than being assembled as kits, the equipment is stored in separate bins for each item and teachers check out the needed supplies, item by item, as required for their instruction.

Evaluate the new endeavor

The overall educational-improvement endeavor should be evaluated in a comprehensive way to aid leaders in improving the process and in laying the groundwork for the new approaches to become a routine and integral part of the school. The evaluation of educational-change efforts should identify both the benefits for students and the quality of the implementation process. Selective measures which only quantify outcomes in a simplistic way will not provide an in-depth understanding of shortcomings and progress. Qualitative studies will be needed, not just conventional tests of student outcomes. Qualitative evaluation studies should also reflect on the interplay of classroom changes and on what was altered inside the school as a whole.

In some settings, specifically schools in the United States, many educators are faced with the task of conducting formal testing of science at the elementary school level. If this is the case, every effort should be made to get the best possible tests that measure a broad range of educational objectives, not just acquisition of lower-level knowledge. More modern performance-oriented assessment methods and instruments have significant potential, although the technical and efficiency problems of such approaches are not inconsequential (see Shavelson & Baxter, 1993). In addition, other means of assessment should be employed, including the use of teachers' professional judgment of the attainment of various objectives and the judging of the products of student work.

Evaluation, of course, is a much broader endeavor than the measuring of student outcomes. It must attend to such matters as teachers' opinions of various aspects of using the program, the process by which the program is initiated and sustained, and the various costs of maintaining it.

TOWARDS ROUTINE: ANCHORING THE NEW— THE INSTITUTIONALIZATION PROCESS

School Personnel	*Administrators* *Support Personnel* *Policy-makers*
• Protect the new • Create organizational identity • Develop ownership and support • Exchange with the public • Link to the school context • Create a solid school identity	• Link to school-leader education • Develop policy programs

Once activity-based learning has been established, school personnel must sustain it. Educational leaders and policy makers should aid school personnel in this nurturing and sustaining. Fostering the spread of this approach into other schools may be part of the task. The following actions are recommended.

Protect the new

A principal or external stakeholder should act to sustain continued use of activity-based learning at a school for which he or she is responsible. As when initiating activity-based learning, the principal who wants to sustain the innovation should protect it against dogmatic opponents. Common to all 15 IMPACT cases is the principals' open commitment and support. It shows up in activities such as the following:

• being an advocate for the new approaches, using experiential knowledge gained from the innovative efforts;

• restructuring time schedules as needed to continue the exchange of experiences among teachers (so important in the implementation stage) and to avoid fragmentation of the established active learning patterns;

• talking with parents to clarify what has been attained thus far, and to communicate the educational value of the new patterns of teaching and learning;

• advocating and promoting both continued self-renewal as important to the school's success and continuation of activity-based learning as an important aspect of unleashing the child's creativity and generating motivation for learning;

• spreading the new practices by setting up teacher teams to support additional implementation and by establishing in-service education courses on the successful work in activity-based learning for teachers in the school.

Create a solid identity for your school

Whatever is changed in a school is perceived and interpreted in different ways by various people, both internally and externally. Especially when new approaches to learning are tested, as in the case of activity-based learning in science, it is important to develop and clarify an educational profile of the school. Vague and uninformed speculation about the goals and direction of the school can be very damaging. It is helpful to take such actions as the following:

• Involve the community in the life of the school to make people aware of the school's new vision and educational ideas.

• Encourage support for the new practices and generate support for future innovative efforts, and permit the public to share a strong sense of identity with your school.

• Explain why the new approach is more effective or meaningful than traditional ways of teaching and learning by inviting the public, policy makers, teachers, and the press to look at what you are doing.

Develop ownership and internal support

Develop ownership and continued support for activity-based learning within the school—without applying pressure—by the following steps:

• Create an open learning climate for children in the school so that everybody gains insight into the new practices without feeling pressure for immediate participation (cf. Anderson, 1982; Hoy, Tarter & Kottkamp, 1991).

• Solicit a climate of reflective openness and sharing of ideas among the staff.

• Reallocate money in the budget toward the development of additional instructional and science curriculum materials.

Attend to the school context

School-based implementation is influenced by both the immediate school culture and by the broader social and political context. The current U.S. situation illustrates several aspects of context. In the broader political arena, for example, there are the rather complementary pushes for well defined educational outcomes, standardized tests, accountability, and even—by some people—for a national curriculum. The person wishing to sustain an established activity-based science program must attend to aspects of these political movements, which are both potentially positive and possibly negative. A possible negative influence of new testing programs, for example, would be to discourage activity-based learning unless the tests can truly measure the full range of student outcomes. Policy-makers must attend to such matters.

On another level, the current context includes a strong push by professionals toward site-based management. Such an orientation is highly compatible with most of the actions taken by schools in our cases. School personnel in such a context probably have increased opportunities for teacher initiative, collegial teacher relationships, and local school decision-making. School leaders may be able to capitalize on the presence of the site-based management philosophy to enhance innovative educational practices.

In one of the U.S. case studies of a school district, a distinct school effect seemed to exist: the message here is that, if the implementation effort is being conducted on a district-wide basis, close attention must be paid to the culture of each individual school and to its current educational goals and instructional approaches. A district-wide program cannot be conducted as if all schools are the same.

Continue staff development

An important aspect of stabilizing new educational working patterns is to educate and assist inexperienced teachers entering the school. Additionally, programs are needed for school-leader education as well. New people are probably entering a context with a different culture than they have experienced in the past. Sustained activity-based learning is part of a school's culture. If the innovative practices are to be sustained, new people must be introduced to the new culture and helped to understand it. The IMPACT cases show that improvement in the classroom and on the school level is to a great extent a social process of learning on all sides. Staff development is an important aspect of this learning, both to sustain what has been acquired and to continue growth toward even better education.

Spread the innovative practice

Policy-makers and educational leaders have reason to want to spread an innovative practice beyond the school where it has been institutionalized. Such a school, in fact, is a major resource for such efforts at spreading innovative practices. Among the steps that can be taken are the following:

- Establish a monitoring system to identify promising projects and examples of activity-based learning. The major task of this system is to make successful practices accessible to other schools or districts. Additionally, a school which showcases such innovative projects or practices is reinforced in its efforts at sustaining exemplary practices.
- Provide some incentives for the uninitiated to consider the new practices and refer them to the information available through the monitoring system and through other means.
- Develop a grants program through which productive schools can apply for resources and support to extend the already established activity-based learning in science. Within such a program, examples of schools with cooperative school climates and good classroom practices can be displayed.

Once activity-based learning has been established in one school, or a portion of a school, there is a foundation from which exciting educational practices can be spread.

References

Adams, R. S., & Biddle, B. J. (1970). *Realities of teaching*. New York: Holt, Rinehart & Winston.

Akker, J. van den (1988). The teacher as learner in curriculum implementation. *Journal of Curriculum Studies, 20*(1), 47-55.

Anderson, C. S. (1982). The search for school climate: A review of the research. *Review of Educational Research, 52*, 368-420.

Anderson, R. D., Anderson, B. L., Varanka-Martin, M. A., Romagnano, L., Bielenberg, J., Flory, M., Mieras, B., Whitworth, J. (1994). *Issues of curriculum reform in science, mathematics and higher order thinking across the disciplines*. Washington, DC: U.S. Government Printing Office.

Averch, H. A., Caroll, Donaldson, Kiesling, & Pincus (1974). *How effective is schooling? A critical review of research*. Englewood Cliffs, NJ: Rand Corporation.

Bashi, J., Sass, Z., Katzir, R., & Margolin, I. (1990). *Effective schools—from theory to practice: An intervention model and its outcomes*. Jerusalem: Van Leer Jerusalem Institute.

Baumert, J. ,Leschinsky, A. (1986). Berufliches Selbstverständnis und Einflußmöglichkeiten von Schulleitern. Ergebnisse einer Schulleiterbefragung. *Zeitschrift für Pädagogik, 32*, 247-266.

Bellack, H., Kliebard, H. M., Hyman, R. T., & Smith, F. L. (1966). *The language of the classroom*. New York: Teachers College Press.

Berg, R., Hameyer, U., & Stokking, K. (1989). *Dissemination reconsidered: The demands of implementation*. (OECD publication). Leuven: Acco.

Berliner, D. C. (1986). In pursuit of the expert pedagogue. *Educational Researcher, 15*(7), 5-13.

Berman, P., Greenwood, P. W., McLaughlin, M. W., & Pincus, J. (1975). *Federal Programs supporting educational change*. Santa Monica, California: Rand Corporation.

Bernstein, B. (1977). *Class, codes and control*. London: Routledge & Kegan Paul.

Bessoth, R. (1983) Kennzeichen effektiver Schulen. In: Bessoth, R. (Ed.), *Schulleiter-Handbuch*. Band 4. Ergänzung Februar 1985. BLK—Bund-Laender-Commission for Educational Planning and Research Promotion: Evaluation von Innovationen im Bereich der Grundschule/Primarschule. Bern: Haupt.

BLK—Bund-Laender-Commission for Educational Planning and Research Promotion: Information. Bonn 1988 (Geschäftsstelle of BLK).

BMBW—Bundesminister für Bildung und Wissenschaft [Federal Ministry of Education and Science]: Grund- und Strukturdaten 1990/91. Bad Honnef 1990 (Bock).

Bredderman, T. (1983). Effects of activity-based elementary science on student outcomes: A quantitative synthesis. *Review of Educational Research, 53*(4), 499-518.

Bredderman, T. (1984). Laboratory programs for elementary school science: A meta-analysis of effects on learning. *Science Education, 69*(4), 577-91.

Caldwell, B. J., & Spinks, J. M. (1988). *The self-managing school*. London, New York, Philadelphia: Falmer Press.

Clark, D. L., Lotto, L. S., & McCarthy, M. M. (1980). Factors associated with success in urban elementary schools. *Phi Delta Kappan, 61*(7), 467-70.

Comber, L. C., & Keeves, J. P., eds. Science education in 19 countries: An empirical study. In *International Studies in Evaluation, 1*. Stockholm: Almquist & Wiksell.

Corbett, H. D., Dawson, J. A. & Firestone, W. A. (1984). *School context and school change*. New York: Teachers College Press.

Crandall, D. & Loucks, S. (1983). A roadmap for school improvement: Executive summary of the study of dissemination efforts supporting school improvement (DESSI). Andover: The NETWORK Inc.

Deutscher Bildungsrat: Strukturplan für das Bildungswesen. Empfehlungen der Bildungskommission. Bonn 1970 (Bundesdruckerei).

DeLucchi, L., Malone, L., & Thier, H. D. (1980). Science activities for the visually impaired: Developing a model. *Exceptional Children, 46*(4), 287-288.

Dreeben, R. (1973) The school as a workplace. In R. M. Travers (Ed.), *Second handbook of research on teaching*. (pp. 450-473). Chicago: MacMillan.

The Educational System in the Federal Republic of Germany. Governance—Structures—Courses. Secretariat of the Standing Conference of Ministers of Education and Cultural Affairs of the Laender. Köln: (DAAD—German Academic Exchange Service) 1982.

Einsiedler, W. & Rabenstein, R. (Eds.). (1985). *Grundlegendes Lernen im Sachunterricht.* Bad Heilbrunn: Klinkhardt.

Einsiedler, W. & Ubbelohde, R. (1985). *Modellversuche im Grundschulbereich.* Bonn: Bund-Laender-Commission for Educational Planning and Research Promotion.

Eisner, E. W. (1970). *The educational imagination.* New York: Macmillan.

Ekholm, M. (1987). The institutionalization of study days in Sweden: A long-term historical review. In M. B. Miles, M. Ekholm, & R. Vandenberghe (Eds.), *Lasting school improvement: Exploring the process of institutionalization.* (OECD publication). (pp. 103-124). Leuven: Acco.

Ekholm, M., & Trier, U. P. (1987). The concept of institutionalization: Some remarks. In M. B. Miles, M. Ekholm, & R. Vandenberghe (Eds.), *Lasting school improvement. Exploring the process of institutionalization.* (pp. 13-21). Leuven: Acco.

Ekholm, M., Hameyer, U., van den Akker, J., & Anderson, R. (Eds.). (1995). *Explorative science learning of 9 to 10 year old children: 15 case studies about successful innovations in four countries.* Kiel: Institute for Science Education, and University of Karlstad).

Ekholm, M. (1987). The institutionalization of study days in Sweden: A longterm historical review. In M. B. Miles, M. Ekholm, & R. Vandenberghe (Eds.), *Lasting school improvement: Exploring the process of institutionalization.* (OECD publication). (pp. 103-124). Leuven: Acco.

Emrick, J. A., & Peterson, S. M. (1978). *A synthesis of findings across five recent studies of educational dissemination and change.* San Francisco: Far West Laboratory.

Erickson, F. (1986). Qualitative methods in research on teaching. In M. C. Wittrock (Ed.), *Handbook of research on teaching* (3rd ed.). (pp. 119-161) New York: Macmillan.

Federal Ministry of Education and Science (Ed.). (1988). *Basic and structural data.* Bad Honnef: Bock.

Fend, H. (1987). »Gute Schulen—Schlechte Schulen«—Die einzelne Schule als pädagogische Handlungseinheit. In U. Steffens, & T. Bargel (Eds.) *Qualität von Schule. Heft 1 der Beiträge aus dem Arbeitskreis »Qualität von Schule«.* (pp. 55-79). Wiesbaden: Hessisches Institut für Bildungsplanung und Schulentwicklung.

Fleming, M. L. (1990). *Elementary teachers' pedagogical beliefs and implicit theories about science.* Unpublished doctoral dissertation, University of Colorado, Boulder.

Fölling-Albers, M. (1989). *Veränderte Kindheit—veränderte Grundschule. Beiträge zur Reform der Grundschule 75.* Frankfurt: Arbeitskreis Grundschule.

Fraser, B. J., Tobin, K., and Lacy, T. (1988). A study of exemplary primary science teachers. *Research in Science and Technological Education,* 6(1), 25-38.

Fraser, B. J. (1986). *Classroom environment.* London: Croomhelm.

Fraser, B. J. (1984). Twenty years of classroom climate work: progress and prospect. *Journal of Curriculum Studies, 21*(4), 307-327.

Frey, K. (1989). *Allgemeine Didaktik.* Zürich: Eidgenössische Technische Hochschule Zürich.

Frey, K. (1984). *Die Projektmethode.* Weinheim: Beltz.

Führ, C. (1989). *Schulen und Hochschulen in der Bundesrepublik Deutschland.* Studien und Dokumentationen zur deutschen Bildungsgeschichte. Köln: Böhlau.

Fullan, M. (1993). *Change forces: Probing the depths of educational reform.* New York: Falmer.

Fullan, M. (1982). *The Meaning of educational change.* Toronto: OISE Press.

Fullan, M. Change processes and strategies at the school level. *The Elementary School Journal, 85*(3), 391-421.

Galton, M., Simon, B., & Croll, P. (1980). *Inside the primary classroom.* London: Routledge & Kegan Paul.

Gaudig, H.: Die Schule der Selbsttätigkeit. Herausgegeben von L. Müller. Heilbrunn 1963 (Klinkhardt).

Gaynor, A. K., Clauset, K. H. (1985). *Implementing and institutianalizing school improvement programs: A theoretical reformulation of the work of Huberman and Miles.* Boston: Boston University.

Good, T. L., & Brophy, J. E. (1986). School effects. In M. C. Wittrock (Ed.), *Handbook of research on teaching.* (3rd ed.). New York: MacMillan.

Goodlad, J. I. (1984). *A place called school.* New York: McGraw-Hill.

Goodlad, J. I. (Ed.). (1987). *The ecology of school renewal.* (Eighty-sixth Yearbook of the Society for the Study of Education Part I). Chicago: University of Chicago Press.

Gross, N., Giaquinta, J. B., & Bernstein, M. (1971). *Implementing organizational innovations: A sociological analysis of planned educational change.* New York: Basic Books.

Haenisch, H. (1987). Was ist eine »gute« Schule? Empirische Forschungsergebnisse und Anregungen für die Schulpraxis. In: U. Steffens, & T. Bargel (Eds.). *Qualität von Schule.* Heft 1 der Beiträge aus dem Arbeitskreis »Qualität von Schule«. (pp. 41-54) Wiesbaden: HIBS.

Hall, G. E., & Loucks, S. F. (1978). Teacher concerns as basis for facilitating and personalizing staff development. *Teachers College Record, 80*(1), 36-53.

Hameyer, U. (1994). Entdeckendes Lernen durch Selbsttaetigkeit. In Hameyer, U., et al., *Pädagogische Ideenkiste Primarbereich.* Kiel: Körner.

Hameyer, U. (1991, April). *Implementing Activity-Based Learning in Elementary Science: Origin, Design, and Current Status of Project* IMPACT. Paper presented at the annual convention of the National Association for Research in Science Teaching, Fontana, WI.

Hameyer, U. (1978). *Innovationsprozesse.* Weinheim: Beltz.

Hameyer, U. ([1978] 1983) *Vier Gesichtspunkte zur Förderung von Innovationsprozessen im Bildungssektor.* Kiel: IPN.

Hameyer, U., Dudek, H., Friis, H. & Hameyer, B.: *Naturwissenschaften AKTIF—Alle Können Teilhaben an Ideen und Fertigkeiten. Lernangebot Sachunterricht und naturwissenschaftliche Fächer* 3. bis 7. Klasse. Kiel [1986](²1992) (Schmidt & Klaunig).

Hameyer, U., & Hameyer, B.: *Kommentarband AKTIF—Alle Können Teilhaben an Ideen und Fertigkeiten.* Lernangebot Sachunterricht und naturwissenschaftliche Fächer 3. bis 7. Klasse. Kiel [1986] (²1992) (Schmidt & Klaunig).

Hameyer, U., Akker, J. van den, Anderson, R. D., Ekholm, M. & Miles, M. (1988). IMPACT *booklet: Implementing activity-based learning in elementary science instruction. A multiple cross-site study.* Kiel: Institute of Science Education at Kiel University.

Hameyer, U., Lauterbach, R., & Wiechmann, J. (Eds.). (1992). *Innovationsprozesse in der Grundschule.* Fallstudien, Analysen und Vorschläge zum Sachunterricht. Bad Heilbrunn: Klinkhardt.

Hedges, L. V., Giaconia, R. M., & Gage, N. L. (1981). *Meta-analysis of the effects of open and traditional instruction.* Stanford University.

Harlen, W. (1985). Science education primary school programs. In T. Husen, & T. N. Postlethwaite (Eds.), *International Encyclopedia of Education.* (pp. 4456-4461) Oxford: Pergamon Press.

Hentig, H. von (1985). *Die Menschen stärken, die Sachen klären.* Stutttgart: Reclam.

Hoy, W. K., Tarter, C. J., & Kottkamp, R. B. (1991). *Open schools—healthy schools: Measuring organizational climate.* London: Sage.

Hoetker, J., & Ahlbrand, P. A., Jr. (1969). The persistence of recitation. *American Educational Research Journal, 6*(2), 145-167. (March).

Huberman, M., & Miles, M. B. (1984). *Innovation up close.* New York: Plenum.

Jacob, E. (1987). Qualitative research traditions: A review. *Review of Educational Research, 57*(1), 1-50.

Joyce, B., Murphy, C., Showers, B., & Murphy, J. (1989). School renewal as cultural change. *Educational Leadership, 47*(3), 70-78.

Kasper, H., & Pichorowski, A. (1978). *Offener Unterricht an Grundschulen.* Langenau-Albeck: Vaas.

Keith, P. M., & Smith, L. M. (1971). *Anatomy of educational innovations: an organizational analysis of an elementary school.* New York/London: John Wiley & Sons.

Klafki, W. (1989). Ziele zeitgemäβer Grundschulpädagogik. *Grundschule,* 2, 25-29.

Klein, M. F. (1991). *The politics of curriculum decision-making.* Albany, NY: State University of New York Press.

Klemm, K. et al. (1990). *Bildungsgesamtplan '90. Ein Rahmen für Reformen.* München: Juventa.

Klemm, K., Böttcher, W., & Weegen, M. (1992). *Bildungsplanung in den neuen Bundesländern.* Entwicklungstrends, Perspektiven und Vergleiche. München: Juventa.

KMK (Konferenz der Kultusminister der Länder der Bundesrepublik Deutschland): Tendenzen und Auffassungen zum Sachunterricht in der Grundschule (Bericht des Schulausschusses). In: Einsiedler, W./Rabenstein, R. (Hrsg.): Grundlegendes Lernen im Sachunterricht. Bad Heilbrunn 1985, 117-125 (Klinkhardt).

Koumin, J. (1970). *Discipline and group management in classrooms.* New York: Holt, Rinehart & Winston.

Kuhlmann, C. (1987). Entdeckendes Lernen und Basisqualifikationen—Entdecken von Wirklichkeiten. In: Hameyer, U. *AKTIF—Erfahrungsberichte und Studien.* (pp. 134-144) Kiel (Institut für die Pädagogik der Naturwissenschaften).

Kyle, W. C. Jr. & Shymansky, J.A. (1988). What research says about teachers as researchers. *Science and Children, 26*(3), 29-31.

Landesinstitut für Schule und Weiterbildung (Hrsg.): Lernen verändert sich—Schulen entwickeln sich. Präsentation von Praxisbeispielen zur Gestaltung des Schullebens und Öffnung von Schule. Soest 1989 (Landesinstitut für Schule und Weiterbildung).

Lay, W. A. (1908). *Experimentelle Pädagogik mit besonderer Rücksicht auf die Erziehung durch die Tat*. Leipzig: Teubner.

Lehming, R. & Kane, M. (1981). *Improving schools. Using what we know*. Beverly Hills, CA: Sage.

Lichtenstein-Rother, I. (1986). Der pädagogische Ort der freien Arbeit in der Regelschule. *Lehrer Journal, 54*(5), 194-197; 198-200.

Little, J. (1981). *The power of organizational setting: school norms and staff development*. Paper presented at the annual meeting of the AERA, Los Angeles, CA.

Louis, K. S. (1983). Dissemination systems: Some lessons from programs of the past. In W. J. Paisley, & M. Butler (Eds.), *Knowledge utilization systems in education*. (pp. 65-88). Beverly Hills, CA: Sage.

Louis, K.S., Rosenblum, S., & Molitor, J.A. (1981). *Strategies for knowledge use and school improvement*. Cambridge, MA: Abt Associates.

Miles, M. B. (1983). Unravelling the mystery of institutionalization. *Educational Leadership, 41*(3), 14-19.

Miles, M. B. & Huberman, A. M. (1984). *Qualitative data analysis: A sourcebook of new methods*. Beverly Hills, CA: Sage.

Miles, M. B., Ekholm, M. (1985). What is school improvement? In W. Van Velzen, M. B. Miles, M. Ekholm, U. Hameyer, & D. Robin (Eds.). *Making school improvement work. A conceptual guide to practice* (pp. 33-67). Leuven: Acco.

Miles, M.B., Velzen, W. van , Ekholm, M., Hameyer, U. & Robin, D. (1985). *Making school improvement work: A conceptual guide to practice*. (OECD publication). Leuven: Acco.

Miles, M.B., Ekholm, M., & Vandenberghe, R. (1987). *Lasting school improvement: Exploring the process of institutionalization*. Leuven: Acco.

Morgan, G. (1993). *Imaginitation: The art of creative imagination*. London: Sage.

Mortimer, P., Sammons, P., Stoll, L., Lewis, D., & Ecob, R. (1988). *School matters: The junior years*. Somerset: Open Books.

Murphy, C. (1983). *Effective principals: Knowledge, talent, spirit of inquiry*. San Francisco.

Neber, H., Wagner, A. C., & Einsiedler, W. (Eds.). (1978). *Selbstgesteuertes Lernen*. Weinheim: Beltz.

Purkey, S. C., & Smith, M. S. (1983). Effective schools: a review. *Elementary School Journal, 83*(4), 427-452.

Ramseger, J. (1977). *Offener Unterricht in der Erprobung: Erfahrungen mit einem didaktischen Modell*. München: Juventa.

Riquarts, K. (1988). *The school system in the Federal Republic of Germany with regard to science education*. Kiel: Institute for Science Education, polycop.

Rolff, H. G., & Zimmermann, P. (1985). *Kindheit im Wandel*. Weinheim: Beltz.

Rutter, M., Maughan, B., Mortimore, P., & Ouston, P. (1980). *Fünzehntausend stunden*. Weinheim: Beltz.

Rutter, M. (1983). School effects on pupil progress: research findings and policy implications. In L. S. Sullivan, & G. Sykes (Eds.), *Handbook of Teaching and Policy*. New York: Longbean.

Sarason, S.B. ([1971] 1982). *The culture of the school and the problem of change*. Boston: Allyn & Bacon.

Schaef, A. W. & Fassel, D. (1988). *The addictive organization*. San Francisco: Harper & Row.

Schlechty, P. C. (1991). *Schools for the 21st century. Leadership imperatives for educational research*. San Francisco: Jossey-Bass.

Schoenberger, M., & Russell, T. (1986). Elementary science as a little added frill: A report of two case studies. *Science Education, 70*(5), 519-538.

Schon, D. A. (1991). *Educating the reflective practitioner: Toward a new design for teaching and learning in the professions*. San Francisco: Jossey-Bass.

Schon, D. A. (1983). *The reflective practitioner: How professionals think in action*. London: Temple Smith.

Schreier, H. (1992). *Entwicklungslinien im Sachunterricht der Primarstufe seit 1980—eine Übersicht zu Forschung, Entwicklung und Erprobung in der Bundesrepublik Deutschland*. Hamburg: Polykopie.

Schwab, J. J. (1978). *Science, curriculum and liberal education: Selected essays*. Chicago: University of Chicago Press.

Shulman, L. S. (1986). Those who understand: Knowledge growth in teaching. *Educational Researcher, 15*(2), 4-14.

Shymansky, S., Kyle, W.C., & Alport, J.M. (1983). The effects of new science curricula on student performance. *Journal of Research on Science Teaching, 20*, 387-404.

Shymansky, J. A., Hedges, L. V., & Woodworth, G. (1990). A Reassessment of the effects of inquiry-based science curricula of the '60s on student performance. *Journal of Research in Science Teaching, 2*, 127-144.

Shymansky, S. & Kyle, W. C. (1991). *Establishing a research agenda: the critical issues of science curriculum reform*. Washington: National Science Foundation.

Sirotnik, K. (1983). What you see is what you get—consistency, persistency, and mediocrity in classrooms. *Harvard Educational Review, 53*, 16-31.

Stake, R. E. (1988). Case study methods in educational research: Seeking sweet water. In Jaeger, R. M. (Ed.), *Complementary methods for research in education*. (pp. 253-276). Washington, D.C.: AERA.

Statistisches Bundesamt (Ed.). (1992). *Bildung im Zahlenspiegel*. Wiesbaden: Metzler-Poeschel.

Steffens, U., & Bargel, T. (Eds.). (1987). *Erkundungen zur Wirksamkeit und Qualität von Schule*. (Heft 1 der Beiträge aus dem Arbeitskreis "Qualität von Schule"). Wiesbaden: HIBS.

Steffens, U., & Bargel, T. (Eds.). (1987). *Fallstudien zur Qualität von Schule*. (Heft 2 der Beiträge aus dem Arbeitskreis "Qualität von Schule"). Wiesbaden: HIBS.

Taylor, S. J., & Bogdan, R. (1984). *Introduction to qualitative research methods: The search for meanings*. New York: Wiley.

Timmermans, R.: Institutionalization of the MAVO project—A Dutch case study. In M. B. Miles, M. Ekholm, & R. Vandenberghe (Eds.), *Lasting school improvement: Exploring the process of institutionalization*. (OECD publication). (pp. 125-142) Leuven: Acco.

Thomas, S. C., & Walberg, H. J. (1975). An analytic review of the literature. In B. Spodek, & H. J. Walberg (Eds.), *Studies in open education*. (pp. 13-41). New York: Agathon Press.

Van den Berg, R., Hameyer, U., & Stokking, K. (1989). *Dissemination reconsidered. Demands from implementation*. Leuven: Acco.

Van Velzen, W. G., Miles, M. B., Ekholm, M., Hameyer, U., & Robin, D. (1985). *Making school improvement work: A conceptual guide to practice*. (OECD publication). Leuven: Acco.

Walberg, H. J. (1991). Improving school science in advanced and developing countries. *Review of Educational Research, 61*(1), 25-69.

Walberg, H. J. (1984). Syntheses of Research on Teaching. In M. C. Wittrock (Ed.), *Handbook of Research on Teaching*. Washington, D.C.: McMillan.

Walberg, H. J. (1988). *Productive teaching and instruction: Assessing the knowledge base*. Chicago: University of Illinois.

Wallrabenstein. W. (1991). *Offener Schule Unterricht*. Reinbek: Rowohlt.

Wallrabenstein, W. (1988) Offener Unterricht kontrovers. In *Die Grundschulzeitschrift*, 2(11), 6-10.

Waterman, R.H. (1988) *Leistung durch Innovation*. Hamburg: Hoffmann & Campe.

Weick, K. (1976). Educational organizations as loosely coupled systems. *Administrative Science Quarterly, 21*, 1-19.

Wiechmann, J. (1991). *Entwicklung einzelner Schulen*: Fallstudie einer Region. Kiel: Vorbereitung.

Yager, R. E. and Penick, J. E. (1983). Analysis of the current problems with school science in the United States of America. *European Journal of Science Education, 5*(4), 463-469.

Yin, R. K. (1987). *Case study research: Design and methods*. Beverly Hills, CA: Sage.

Index